Nathanael West

Literature and Life Series
[Formerly Modern Literature
and World Dramatists]

Selected list of titles:

Complete list of titles in the series available from publisher on request.

Nathanael West

Robert Emmet Long

FREDERICK UNGAR PUBLISHING CO.
New York

Copyright © 1985 by Frederick Ungar Publishing Co., Inc.

Library of Congress Cataloging in Publication Data
Long, Robert Emmet.
 Nathanael West.

 (Literature and life series)
 Bibliography: p.
 Includes index.
 1. West, Nathanael, 1903–1940–Criticism and interpre-
tation. I. Title. II. Series.
PS3545.E8334Z755 1985 813'.52 84-24488
ISBN 0-8044-2543-4

Printed and bound in Great Britain by
Biddles Ltd, Guildford and King's Lynn

For Roger Austen

Contents

Chronology

1903   Nathan Weinstein ("Nathanael West") born October 17, first child and only son of Anna (Wallenstein) and Max Weinstein, successful building contractor in New York City.

1908–1917   Attends public schools in New York City, reads precociously but often absent from classes, and receives poor grades.

1917–1920   Attends DeWitt Clinton High School, New York City, an inconspicuous student often absent from classes; does not graduate. Spends summers at Camp Paradox in the Adirondacks, where receives nickname "Pep," due to apparent lack of vitality.

1921   With "doctored" high school transcript, enters Tufts College; fails all his courses, and has to leave at the end of first semester.

1922–1924   Transfers to Brown University using transcript of another Nathan Weinstein, whose advanced credits enable him to graduate in two and a half years. S. J. Perelman, also at Brown, becomes close friend.

1925–1926   Intermittently employed in father's construction business, while reading widely and making early efforts at writing. August 1926 legally changes name to Nathanael

West. October–January in Paris. Called
home as parents' prosperity declines, due to
slump in building trade.

1927–1929   Relatives arrange job as night manager at
Kenmore Hall Hotel, New York City,
where he begins early draft of *Balso Snell*. In
1929, sister Laura marries S. J. Perelman,
and through them meets Edmund Wilson,
and circle of writers for *The New Yorker*.

1930–1932   Becomes manager of the Sutton Hotel,
where provides free lodging for indigent
writer friends, including James T. Farrell,
Lillian Hellman, and Dashiell Hammett.
The Dream Life of Balso Snell published in
spring 1931, in limited edition of five hundred
copies. Friendship with William Carlos
Williams; becomes associate editor of his
"little magazine" *Contact*, 1931–32.

1933   With the Perelmans, becomes co-owner of
farmhouse, Erwinna, Pennsylvania. *Miss
Lonelyhearts* published by Liveright to
enthusiastic reviews; but firm goes bankrupt,
and sales of book are meager. Associate
editor of satirical magazine *Americana*,
which survives less than a year. First assignment in Hollywood, as script writer for
Columbia Pictures.

1934   Returns to Erwinna. *A Cool Million*
published to poor sales and reviews.
Collaborates with Perelman on unproduced
play *Even Stephen*. Applies for Guggenheim
fellowship, with recommendations by F.
Scott Fitzgerald, Edmund Wilson, and
Malcolm Cowley, but is turned down.

1935   Returns to Hollywood to seek employment
as screenwriter, and experiences discouraging

	period of unemployment, poverty, and illness.
1936–1938	Employed as script writer for low-budget films with Republic Pictures. Works on *The Day of the Locust*, and collaborates with Joseph Schrank on antiwar play, *Good Hunting*, which closes on Broadway, November 1938, after two performances.
1939	*The Day of the Locust* published by Random House. Period of better-paid script work for a number of studios. Hunting trips with William Faulkner and others.
1940	Marries Eileen McKenney April 19. Friendship in Hollywood with F. Scott Fitzgerald. Collaborates with Boris Ingster on highly-paid "original" movie scripts. December 22, is killed with wife in auto crash near El Centro, California, returning from hunting trip in Mexico.
1957	*The Complete Works of Nathanael West*, in one volume, published to critical acclaim; West revival begins.

Nathanael West: The Shape of the Life

Nathanael West was an original, disturbing novelist of ruthless satiric gifts, and one of the most talented prose writers to appear in the 1930s. Because he died young, at thirty-seven, he left behind only a small body of work, four slender novels published between 1931 and 1939; but his importance cannot be measured by the number or length of the books he wrote. The English critic Cyril Connolly has compared West's *Miss Lonelyhearts* to Fitzgerald's *The Great Gatsby* and Hemingway's *The Sun Also Rises* as one of the three most perfect novels produced in this century; and even after much time has passed, *The Day of the Locust* continues to be regarded as the best of the novels that have been written about Hollywood. West was essentially a comic writer, but in the sense that Kafka and Gogol are, in their imaginings of a real yet baffling and fantastic world. West's was the comedy of pain, of radical social and moral alienation, and in this respect he charted "the territory ahead."

When Nathan Weinstein legally changed his name to Nathanael West, he adopted a deeply ambiguous identity. The two parts of the assumed name imply contradictions that beset the man—the New England "Nathanael" (an elegant variation of Nathaniel), with its intimations of a secure place within an established cultural order, versus a Californian "West," that is formless and synonomous with dreams of newly-monied "success." A conflict of identity went far back in West's own past.[1] His parents, of German-Jewish origin, had lived in the Lithuanian section of Russia in the latter part of the nineteenth century. His mother, Anna Wallenstein, belonged to a family of some consequence, since her father was a builder of railroad stations all along the Hamburg–St. Petersburg line; the Weinsteins were less highly placed, but were at least solidly middle class, and they too earned their livelihoods in the building trades. During the Russification of Lithuania in the 1880s, however, intense pressures were brought to bear on the German community, particularly on German Jews; and not even the solid bourgeois status of the Wallensteins spared them the many restrictions (of vocation and even travel) that affected the Jewish settlement. As these restrictions steadily increased, a number of the younger Wallensteins and Weinsteins managed to emigrate to New York City. Sometime around 1890, Max Weinstein, West's father, joined his older brothers on the Lower East Side, and before long he began to prosper as a building contractor. By 1902 he was responsible for many of the new apartment buildings in Harlem and the Upper West Side. It was during that year that he married Anna Wallenstein. Nathan, their first child and only son, was born in 1903; and his two sisters, Hinda and Laura, were born, respectively, in 1904 and 1911.

The family moved frequently, occupying an apartment in one new building after another that Max Weinstein had built on the West Side. Already prospering, the Weinsteins were anxious to succeed in their new environment, to become "Americanized" immediately. Differentiating themselves from the *shtetl* community of Jews on the Lower East Side, they did not speak Yiddish or Russian. Instead, they taught their children German and learned English themselves. They attended a German synagogue when they attended one at all—usually twice a year, on high holidays. Nathan Weinstein was never sent to Hebrew schools, received little or no education in the Jewish religion, and was never confirmed in a Bar Mitzvah ceremony. There was thus, in their household, a certain ambiguousness. The Weinsteins were Jewish, yet they stood apart from the mainstream of American Jewish life; and this uncertainty of status must surely have affected Nathan Weinstein's sense of himself even at an early age.

His sense of identity was complicated further by conflicts of clan loyalty that existed within the family. Anna Wallenstein and her relatives cultivated a sense of superiority based on the earlier social position of the Wallensteins in Europe, and their association with solid German "culture," extending even to a presumption of kinship with Wallenstein himself, the hero of Schiller's famous play. The Weinsteins, successful achievers in New York, were associated in this equation with merely practical and commercial endeavors. If the Wallensteins represented a lost romantic past, the Weinsteins stood for a money-oriented American present. One of the father's earliest gifts to his son was a set of the Horatio Alger books; but the Wallensteins, and particularly the mother, impressed on the boy's mind an idea of superiority to the American capitalist society into which they were still anxious to be assimilated.

As a boy, Nathan Weinstein was an avid and precocious reader of books, and is even supposed to have kept a toy bulldog in his room to prevent members of his family from disturbing his reading. He would not or could not take his place with the other boys, and was frequently absent from school, PS 81, on 119th Street and St. Nicholas Avenue, just around the corner from their house. As a result, he received poor grades during his seven years in the school. One wonders why his parents permitted, as they evidently did, his unusual behavior, and can only conclude that he was regarded as an exceptional child who must be indulged. By his absence from his classes, Nathan was a kind of "home child," even a kind of preschooler, kept small and protected. Ironically, he asserted his superiority early in unusually passive behavior and through a vivid imaginative life.

In 1917 he registered for DeWitt Clinton High School, a good academic high school in a poor district on Tenth Avenue and 59th Street. Here again he was often absent from his classes, received markedly poor grades, and did not participate in school activities. Few of his contemporaries at DeWitt Clinton, including Lionel Trilling, later remembered ever having met him. His summers were spent at a boys' camp in the Adirondacks, which emphasized sports at which Nathan, a thin, ungainly, and awkward boy, did not excel. He tried out for baseball, but was the sort of boy who, in fielding a fly, would be struck by the ball on the forehead and fall to the ground, which did, in fact, once happen to him. Others at the camp remember him as being anemic and listless and gave him the lasting nickname of "Pep," for his apparent lack of energy. In turn, Nathan Weinstein drew mocking caricatures of the other campers and their activities. When DeWitt Clinton reopened in the fall of 1919, he did not report for his senior year.

What Nathan did do that year was to forge a transcript of his grades—making erasures and raising his marks— which admitted him to Tufts College in the fall of 1921. At Tufts he rarely went to class, and received such poor grades that by the end of the first semester he was required to leave. Before leaving, however, he applied as a transfer student to Brown University, and apparently arranged to have the transcript of another Nathan Weinstein at Tufts substituted for his own. On the strength of this transcript, he was promptly admitted to the Ivy League college for its spring 1922 term. The transcript of the other Nathan Weinstein, moreover, was quite impres-

sive, with fifty-seven credits earned in Chemistry, Biol-
ogy, Physics, and Economics, which exempted West
from required courses at Brown and enabled him to
graduate in two and a half years.

A fabricator of transcripts, West arrived at Brown
with a fabricated background, telling his fellow students
that he had served in the US Navy. Later in life, he continued to relate romantic stories about himself, including
the distinct fiction that he had played on the Brown University baseball team. His manner of dress at Brown set
him apart from others and was possibly meant to match
the story he gave out that his people had been of "gentle
birth" in Europe. Philip Lukin, his roommate, has
described him in the following way: "He was meticu-
lously clothed in the then current fashion which meant
Brooks Brothers suits, argyle socks, Whitehouse and
Hardy brogues, Brooks shirts and ties and Herbert
Johnson or Lock and Co. hats. One might assume that he
was a dandy when it came to clothes and one would
assume that this was an attempt to compensate for his lack
of other [attractive] physical attributes." That West
regarded himself as being physically unattractive comes
up again in the recollection of others who knew him at
that time. Jeremiah Mahoney remarked that West and his
friend Brae Rafferty "made a quaint looking pair. Both
were slender; both had sallow, rather coarse and faintly
blemished skin, prominent noses, long heads, and a taste
for similar clothing—the homburg, the funereal overcoat, the Brooks suit. Together, strolling down College
Hill, they resembled a couple of well-heeled mortuary
assistants."

Despite the oddness of his dress, West was well liked
at college. Although shy and reserved, he had a gift for
blending in well with others. In his social life, however,
he was unfortunate in at least one respect. He was
strongly attracted to the college fraternities and desper-

ately wished to be pledged, but since none of them
accepted Jews, he was excluded from membership.
Oddly, he spent quite a bit of time at the fraternity
houses, including one that was the most notoriously anti-
Semitic on campus; and one would suspect a certain
masochism in his frequent presence at these houses where
he was accepted in a certain way but not wanted as a
member. Some of those who knew him have claimed that
his experience of exclusion left lasting scars. After leaving
Brown, West attempted to disavow his Jewishness
which, according to his friend John Sanford, he regarded
as a "curse." He cultivated markedly conservative manners and dress, and changed his name from Nathan
Weinstein to the Brahmanish Nathanael West. He
avoided Jewish girls, whom he called "bagels," and eventually married a gentile. None of his heroes are Jews, and
three of the four are New England WASPs.

The college yearbook of 1924 identified West as a
genius with an unpredictable future. His scholastic performance was unexceptional, but less formally he distin-
guished himself as an omnivorous reader, and owned the
largest personal library of books of any student at Brown.
He read Eliot, Pound, Yeats, and the French Symbolists;
and knew Flaubert and Dostoyevsky especially well. He
was drawn to Nietzsche, discovered Joyce, read much of
Anatole France, and was the first student at Brown to
read James Branch Cabell's *Jurgen*. The literature that
engaged him most was the offbeat, the bizarre, and the
morbid. He explored mysticism and medieval Catholi-
cism, read Huysmans's *À Rebours* and Arthur Machen's
The Hill of Dreams, each of which takes the hero to the
outer limits of sanity and beyond.

West's most important student association at Brown
was with S. J. Perelman,[2] then attracting attention as a
cartoonist and humorist. West himself sketched and drew
cartoons and designed the first cover for *Casements*, the

college literary magazine to which he contributed poetry and an essay on Euripides. In class, instead of taking notes, he sometimes wrote the name "Nathan von Wallenstein Weinstein" over and over, as if lost in a private dream world; and at other times he did religious doodles, sketches of suffering saints, and martyrs. He also wrote comic-grotesque religious parodies, which were later incorporated into *The Dream Life of Balso Snell*—the passages that deal with St. Puce, a flea who lived under the armpit of Christ, and Maloney the Areopagite, who seeks to emulate Christ's agony by crucifying himself with thumbtacks.

After graduating, West returned to New York to live with his family and worked intermittently in his father's construction business. Of the members of his immediate family, he was particularly close to his younger sister Laura, who was interested in writing and had an "alert, witty, and questioning mind"; and his father, a thin, pale, modest man whom West resembled physically. West's mother had once been a beautiful girl, courted in Europe by the noted painter Maurice Stern, but by the 1920s, according to James F. Light, she had become heavy and had settled into the role of "the typically *Yiddische hausfrau*, kindly enough and devoted to her family but dominating."[3] Max Weinstein, a gentle and sympathetic man, is said to have been dominated by her, and it would seem that West was. His ambivalent attitude toward women was no doubt incubated in the Weinstein household; it is suggested, at least, in his vaguely incestuous remark that he could not marry a woman who did not resemble Laura and his mother. Most women, seemingly, did not, for West arrived at Brown already suffering from gonorrhea, and contracted it again during his first year. He had apparently contracted the infection from prostitutes who stood, in his mind, at the far extreme from his mother, in the defilement he attributed to them. In college, indeed, he would quote Odo of Cluny's reference to the female as a "saccus stercoris," or sac of filth; but his mother and Laura were presumably exempt from this stricture.

By the summer of 1926, West was set upon going to Paris, a project opposed at first by his family because of the recent decline in the construction business; but the parents eventually relented and agreed to support him abroad for a limited time. In August of that year he had his name legally changed (a number of his cousins had changed their names also) to Nathanael West, as if adopting a new identity for his trip abroad. West left for Paris in October, but his period there, if important, was not extremely eventful. He lived modestly on the fringe of Montparnasse, visited sidewalk cafés like the Deux Magots, which was evoked vividly in Hemingway's recently published *The Sun Also Rises*, and haunted Sylvia Beach's Shakespeare and Co. bookshop, where he bought many books, including several copies of *Ulysses*. He caught glimpses of Cocteau, Gide, and Hemingway, and acquainted himself further with the work of the Dadaists and Surrealists. But as economic conditions worsened at home, West's anxious parents entreated him to return, and he reluctantly came back to America—less than three months after he had arrived in Paris. Later, he would embellish upon his brief stay, telling friends, and even permitting it to be stated on the jacket of *Miss Lonelyhearts*, that he had been an expatriate in Paris for two years. He sometimes told heartbreaking stories to credulous listeners of his destitution in Paris in the course of a bohemian existence. None of these stories had any basis in fact.

On his return to New York, relatives found him employment as night manager of the Kenmore Hall Hotel, on East 23rd Street, a marginal establishment with small, low-rent rooms, and a drugstore fountain rather

than a restaurant. Here, while playing the businessman,
West dreamed the bizarre dreams of the unconscious
recorded in *Balso Snell*. Friends of this time recall him as
being "gentle" and "sympathetic"; but others were conscious of a complicated nature. Robert Coates implies
that West possessed not one but two selves—one genial,
sociable, tactful, and considerate; the other quite
detached and deeply pessimistic.[4] Josephine Herbst and
her husband John Herrmann, who had published first
novels and were introduced to West by William Carlos
Williams, found West elusive and puzzling. Herbst
speaks of his poise and graciousness, yet saw in his eyes
some mystery of "emotions beyond explanation," making her think of some long lost child.[5]

In 1927 West brought his friend S. J. Perelman to meet
his parents, who then lived on West 79th Street, and two
years later his sister Laura and Perelman were married.
With Perelman's first book about to be published, they
moved to an apartment near Washington Square, and
West was a frequent visitor, finding in the Perelmans a
kind of "second family." Through them, too, he was
introduced to a circle of writers for *The New Yorker*,
which included Dorothy Parker, George S. Kaufman,
James Thurber, and Alexander Woolcott. Other writers
living in Greenwich Village whom he came to know at
this time included Edmund Wilson and Malcolm Cowley. But West's own status as a writer was uncertain. His
aspirations were opposed, for reasons of prudence, by his
family, and at the Kenmore he wrote short stories that
were either never finished or were rejected by magazines.
His nouvelle, *The Dream Life of Balso Snell*, was written
and rewritten over a period of four years. The book was
eventually published by David Moss and Martin Kamin,
whose midtown bookstore West frequented and whom
he had come to know personally. Moss and Kamin had
just taken over the Contact Edition series from Robert

McAlmon, who had published avant-garde, experimental writers in the series during the 1920s. Their reader for the manuscript was William Carlos Williams,[6] who recommended its publication strongly and soon became a friend of West's. *The Dream Life of Balso Snell* appeared in the spring of 1931 in an edition of five hundred copies (with the sale of the first 150 guaranteed by the author), the profits from which can be imagined.

In December 1930, again through his family's contacts, West became manager of the Sutton Club Hotel, on East 56th Street, which soon became a gathering place of his writer friends. The Sutton almost always had vacant rooms, and with a generosity that was typical of him, West allowed many of his friends to occupy them. The Perelmans lived in the hotel at one point, and West's friend John Sanford stayed there for five months. Quentin Reynolds (West's classmate at Brown), Edmund Wilson, and Robert Coates all lived there at one time or another. When James T. Farrell and his wife were evicted from their hotel, West gave them rooms for two weeks; and Erskine Caldwell, Lillian Hellman, and Dashiell Hammett[7] were provided with rooms at the hotel when they were without means. The Sutton also proved a rich source for West's imagination, since its tenants came to seem a microcosm of the displaced and "unsuccessful" in American society. Noting their attempts to present a genteel façade, and sensing the desperation beneath it, he became fascinated with their inner lives. At times he even went so far as to steam open their mail. West's conception of pervasive human misery in *Miss Lonelyhearts* was almost certainly affected by his empathetic-voyeuristic interest in the hotel's tenants.

Miss Lonelyhearts was written very slowly and revised endlessly over a period of almost four years. During the summer of 1931, West took a leave of absence from the hotel to work exclusively on the novel at a cabin in the Adirondacks; and he later left the hotel again to prepare the final draft at a small hotel in Frenchtown, New Jersey. Even after the book was accepted, he rewrote it in galleys, eliminating lines, condensing it, and making scores of minute improvements. *Miss Lonelyhearts* was published in the spring of 1933 by Liveright, and received exceptionally favorable reviews, even becoming the subject of a critical symposium in the little magazine *Contempo*.[8] In advance of publication, and included on the jacket of the book, Edmund Wilson wrote that *Miss Lonelyhearts* "is not in the least like the work of even the best American humorous writers because Mr. West has a philosophic-poetic point of view which our humor usually lacks. . . . Though he has evidently been influenced by the irony of Dada, he strains less and goes deeper than Dada. Mr. West is, in short, an original comic poet; and he has made . . . a miniature comic epic." Comments of reviewers were hardly less enthusiastic. John Preston commented that *Miss Lonelyhearts* "is a brilliantly witty and ironic picture of Dostoyevsky's 'Poor People' transferred to the chaos of New York in the present century," and Robert Coates, in *The New Yorker*, spoke of West's style as "a prose that is like glass for transparency and that is lit by the most fantastic and colorful imagination."

The Liveright edition was limited to only 2,200 copies, but with the reviews the book received West should have been immediately considered a writer with a reputation and a following. Instead, he met with bitter disappointment and frustration. Just as the book was published, Liveright went bankrupt, and the printers confiscated most of the copies of the book, holding them until payment had been secured. For months efforts were made to release the copies, but when they were finally made available for sale, reviews of the book were all but forgotten, and it sold poorly. The story of the publication of *Miss Lonelyhearts* reads like an absurdly cruel joke that West might have appreciated had he not been its victim.

Improbably, since the novel's pessimism would seem to preclude it for film adaptation,[9] Twentieth Century Pictures purchased *Miss Lonelyhearts* as a screen property, a sale that was accompanied by an offer from Columbia Pictures to write an original screenplay. West then went to Hollywood, where he worked on an unproduced film and remained to write another. When he returned East at the end of the year, repelled yet in some sense fascinated by the underside of life in Los Angeles that he had seen (its many peripheral people, variously deformed and with many sexual quirks), he told a cousin that "a trip to Hollywood was like a ride in a glass-bottomed boat in the waters near Bermuda, where you see garish, improbable fauna swimming about."[10]

In New York, at the end of the summer of 1933, West joined Gilbert Seldes and George Grosz as associate editor of *Americana*,[11] a magazine that satirized almost every aspect of American life in the thirties. West was influential in putting together its Hollywood issue, but with that number the magazine folded, and he then went to live at a farmhouse near Erwinna, in Bucks County, Pennsylvania. During the previous year Josephine Herbst and John Herrmann had urged West to settle in their region, recommending it as a place where he could write in tranquil surroundings. Their neighbor Mike Gold, the Marxist novelist and editor, offered his farmhouse for sale for only six thousand dollars, and in December 1932 West, with the Perelmans, made a down payment on it. Now anxious to begin his third novel, West settled into the house, which was shared at times by Laura and S. J. Perelman. Occasionally there were visitors from New York, notably Dashiell Hammett, Lillian Hellman, Robert Coates, and Edmund Wilson. But West's "permanent" house guest was his mother, left a widow the year before.

Anna Weinstein has been described by West's first biographer, James F. Light, as a heavyset woman who dismissed her son's literary aspirations as impractical dreams, even after the critical acclaim for *Miss Lonelyhearts*. "West almost feared his mother," Light remarks, "a woman who, apparently, wallowed in suffering and who gained much pleasure from nagging. Her needs were constantly in the back of West's mind. If he stopped in for an evening visit with the Herrmanns, who lived hardly a hundred yards away, he always remembered to call 'Mama' if he stayed a little late. If he dropped in for an afternoon, he always remembered when dinner time came, and no matter how stimulating the occasion, he left for dinner at home 'because Mama had fussed over it so.' Once, because of a tardy train, the Herrmanns were late for a dinner date with West and his mother. The sorrowful complaints of Mrs. Weinstein were vivid and lengthy."[12] Light quotes a close friend of West's as saying that West "was monopolized by a possessive mother and quite unable, at the time, to free himself from this thralldom."[13]

This "thralldom" is particularly interesting in view of West's relationship to at least two young women during the early thirties. In the winter of 1929–30, he was introduced by the Perelmans to the Paris fashions writer for *The New Yorker*, Beatrice Matthieu, who had come to New York for a visit. When they met, they were immediately attracted to each other, and West before long talked of marriage. After Beatrice Matthieu returned to Paris, West wrote to her of his coming to join her, but he hesitated, and postponed the trip indefinitely until she passed out of his life. In view of his uncertain circumstances his failure to follow through is understandable; yet a suggestion remains that some more subterranean fear was involved in his inability to act.

A year later West met Alice Shepard, the "A. S." to

whom *Balso Snell* is dedicated. Alice was a classmate of Laura's at Pembroke College, a tall, attractive woman, and the chief fashion model for Elizabeth Hawes. Before long West and Alice were seeing each other regularly, often in the company of the Perelmans, and in the following year West began carrying a blank application for a wedding license in his wallet. But by the next winter the informal engagement was broken suddenly. What happened was that after attending a party West drove Alice and another young woman uptown, dropping Alice off at Grand Central Station, where she took a train to her home in New Rochelle, and he then spent the night with the other woman. Alice, meanwhile, feeling vaguely uneasy, called West late that evening and found that he was not in his room. Inevitably, she confronted West, learned the truth, and ended the relationship. West's behavior is unaccountable if he seriously wished to marry; and it would seem as if, on some level of consciousness, he had wanted to back out of the informal engagement. His attitude toward women was decidedly wary and ambivalent, suggesting inner stress like that suffered by the male characters in his fiction who are brought to psychic crises by women and who experience panic and helplessness. In certain cases, these characters are intimated to struggle with a latent homosexuality.

At Erwinna, West pursued an interest that placed him securely in an all-male bastion, that of small-game hunting—an interest giving him an apparent masculine identity that he had always lacked on the athletic field. He was also kept busy by a number of literary projects, through which he desperately attempted to find a source of income. One was a play written in collaboration with Perelman that was originally entitled *Guardian Angel*, and finally *Even Stephen*. The heroine of the play is a female novelist, Diana Breed Latimer, who appears at a New England girls' college to complete her current book, an exposé of sexual misconduct among college girls, and is soon followed to the campus by her publisher Marcel Schwartz. As complications develop, writers and publishers, newspapermen and publicists, professors and their wives are all lampooned. *Even Stephen*, which owes much more to the humor of Perelman than to West, was completed and submitted to producers, and for a while West was hopeful that he would find an income from the theater. But the script attracted no interest, and the project was dropped.

With his future deeply uncertain, West applied for a Guggenheim fellowship, with supporting recommendations from F. Scott Fitzgerald, Malcolm Cowley, Edmund Wilson, and West's Bucks County neighbor George S. Kaufman. West had not then met Fitzgerald, but had been indirectly befriended by him only a short time before when, in a 1934 preface to the Modern Library reissue of *The Great Gatsby*, Fitzgerald had pointed to West specifically as a young American writer "being harmed . . . for lack of a public." West wrote to Fitzgerald, who responded with a letter to the Guggenheim committee recommending West as a "potential leader in the field of prose fiction." In other supporting letters, Cowley stressed "the brilliant quality" of West's writing, and Wilson characterized West as "a very finished writer." Yet despite these endorsements, his application was turned down. Seemingly rejected everywhere, West devoted the principal part of his time at Erwinna to completing his third novel, *A Cool Million*, a grotesque satire of the Horatio Alger myth of success. *A Cool Million* was published in June 1934 by a small new firm, Covici-Friede, which took a chance on West's book and lost. Reviews were decidedly unfavorable, and very few copies of the novel were sold. In the fall of 1934, West estimated that the royalties from his three novels amounted to only 780 dollars.

In a surprising development, however, Columbia Pictures purchased *A Cool Million* as a screen property,[14] and West was again drawn to Hollywood. He went in the belief that with his novel sale he would be able to find employment as a screenwriter; but once there no work was forthcoming. Living on money lent to him by Perelman, West stayed at a seedy apartment hotel called the Pa-Va-Sed, on North Ivar Street, near Hollywood Boulevard. Its other tenants included unemployed former vaudevillians, who hoped to find work in films, bit players, stunt men, and several midgets. Not only was West alone and impoverished, but before long he also became ill—specifically, with gonorrhea complicated by a congested prostrate gland. Treatment was long, drawn out, and so painful that West could sit in a chair for no more than ten minutes at a time, and was unable to sleep at night. For a time he was cared for by one of the midgets, then by a blonde female bit player who was also a part-time prostitute.

After a year of unemployment, in January 1936, West finally signed a contract with Republic Pictures, at a salary of two hundred dollars a week on a week-to-week trial basis which, after six months, was increased to 250 dollars a week. The Republic assignment was one of the least attractive in the industry, since the company's productions were invariably low-budget films designed for quick consumption and destined for oblivion. Contract writers were kept constantly busy in the Republic mill, moving from one script to another; and during his two years with the studio, West worked on a dozen different films, sometimes in collaboration with other writers, and with a hand in many others. For a writer who labored for four years over a single short novel, West proved surprisingly facile in turning out scripts. But he did not take them seriously, and they have little claim to significance.[15]

When West returned to Los Angeles, he was already thinking of writing a novel about Hollywood; and while there, he became an observer and explorer of Hollywood's offbeat life. He knew the bars and the people who frequented them along Hollywood Boulevard, and was often at Stanley Rose's Hollywood Boulevard bookstore. Rose was a colorful character who had never gone beyond the fourth grade; he had once been in prison, yet had later become a Hollywood agent. In the rear of his bookshop he opened a room where art exhibitions were held and writers gathered in its club-like atmosphere. In addition to West these writers included, at various times, Horace McCoy, William Saroyan, Erskine Caldwell, Dashiell Hammett, F. Scott Fitzgerald, and John O'Hara. Through Rose, West was also introduced to what Lillian Hellman called the "whorish, drunk, dope-taking world" of North Hollywood. With Rose, he met small-time gangsters, went to boxing matches, and to illegal cockfights in the Hollywood hills. He also explored the Mexican-American enclave of the city and seems to have known smugglers who operated back and forth between Mexico and Southern California. It was in this way that he acquired the insider's knowledge of the anomic underside of Hollywood that informs *The Day of the Locust*.

He need not, however, have stepped far beyond the Pa-Va-Sed apartment building to have caught the flavor of lower-depths Hollywood in the mid-thirties. During this time, West told a friend of a scene he had recently witnessed: "He said he was coming home about three or four in the morning, walking down a dim corridor to his apartment, when he heard screaming and yelling and cursing in a woman's voice. Suddenly the door opposite opened and one of the prostitutes whom he happened to know, and knew was a prostitute, said something like 'You goddam son of a bitch, get out of here,' and kicked something out of the door that looked like a dirty bundle of laundry. It started rolling down the hall and suddenly it got up and walked off."[16] In *The Day of the Locust* a similar incident introduces Abe Kusich, a character inspired by a well-known dwarf who peddled papers for years on the corner of North Hollywood and Wilcox Street.

Before leaving for Hollywood, West had been marginally involved in left-wing politics in New York. He had attended meetings of the John Reed Club, which for many members was a preparatory step to membership in the Communist Party; and with his friend James T. Farrell had picketed Ohrbach's, been arrested, and had spent the night in the same jail cell as Edward Dahlberg. But in Hollywood, West's political involvement was accelerated to the degree that he has been called a fellow traveler of the Communist Party. The atmosphere in which he lived in Hollywood in the mid-to-late thirties was tremendously politicized, and many of West's writer friends, including Lillian Hellman and Dashiell Hammett, were far to the left politically. With his usual generosity, West lent his name to a number of causes, signed the manifesto of the 1935 American Writers Congress, which proclaimed "the decay of capitalism [and] the inevitability of revolution," and worked actively for the Spanish Loyalist cause. He was a member of the Screen Writers Guild, an organization in which a remarkable Communist influence existed, and by 1939 was on its executive board. He may, as his biographer, Jay Martin, maintains, have been acting under the stimulus of the political persuasion of friends and may even have felt guilt that he was not more committed than he was. In any case it is evident that if West thought of himself as being a leftist, "fashionable" or otherwise, leftist critics did not. They dismissed his work consistently as socially "irrelevant."

In the spring of 1938 West was hired by RKO Pictures

at 350 dollars a week, an indication that he was beginning to be recognized within the industry, and that it was the start of better times for him financially. He also collaborated with Joseph Schrank on an antiwar play, a black comedy entitled *Good Hunting*, which was presented on Broadway in November 1938 but closed after only two performances.[17] West was chiefly occupied with *The Day of the Locust*, however, which took shape slowly and evolved through a number of separate drafts. By spring 1938 Random House accepted the novel, which was published in the following year. Before it appeared, West showed proofs of the work to F. Scott Fitzgerald who, West said in a letter, "raved . . . about the book." Malcolm Cowley, who also saw the proofs, thought it "wonderful . . . even better than *Miss Lonelyhearts*." When it appeared, reviews were exceptionally favorable, but once again West was thwarted since the novel, which was regarded as bizarre and unwholesome, did not sell.

If West was never able to support himself as a novelist, he did enjoy a measure of commercial success at the end of his life in his Hollywood studio work. With Boris Ingster, he sold two free-lance screen scenarios for ten thousand and twenty-five thousand dollars respectively and bought a house in the Hollywood hills. As often as possible he went on hunting vacations, sometimes with William Faulkner (who admired *Miss Lonelyhearts*, and was then doing screen writing in Hollywood) or with other writers. Most importantly he met his future wife, Eileen McKenney, who had come from the East to work in the promotion and story department of one of the studios and who, before meeting West, had dated John O'Hara. Eileen McKenney had already achieved some celebrity as the subject of her sister Ruth's popular memoir *My Sister Eileen*. She was divorced, with a small child, and had had a life that was much less happy than the ebullient evocation of her in the memoir had implied. It was quite possibly her vulnerability that elicited West's attraction to her. For the first time in his life, at the far end of the continent from his dominating mother, West was able to commit himself emotionally to a woman. West and Eileen were married in Beverly Hills in April 1940, and from all reports their marriage appears to have been a happy one.

During the autumn of 1940, the Wests spent evenings with F. Scott Fitzgerald and his companion Sheila Graham, and a friendship began to develop between the two writers. West may well have spoken to Fitzgerald of his plans for a new novel,[18] but that novel was never to be written. In December the Wests drove to Mexico for a hunting vacation, and on their return, on December 22nd, at El Centro, California (near San Diego) they were involved in a fatal auto accident. A notoriously poor driver, who daydreamed or looked at his passengers while he talked rather than at the road before him, West ran a stop sign and crashed into a car ahead of him. Both West and Eileen died of skull fractures—within twenty-four hours of F. Scott Fitzgerald's death, from a heart attack, in Hollywood.

At the time of his death, West was so little known to the general public that he was identified in newspaper announcements of the crash as a Hollywood screenwriter, with greater prominence given to Eileen McKenney. Summing up, after the accident, Edmund Wilson wrote that West "left two books more finished and complete as works of art than almost anything else produced by his generation,"[19] yet West continued to be an esteemed but largely unread writer. In 1946, *Miss Lonelyhearts* was translated into French by Marcelle Sibon as *Mademoiselle Coeur-Brisé*, with an introduction by the surrealist writer Philippe Soupault, and it created a wave of interest in Nathanael West in France; and in the US, *Miss Lonelyhearts* and *The Day of the Locust* were reprinted by New Directions in the late forties and early fifties. It was not until *The Collected Works of Nathanael West* was published in 1957, however, that the West revival began. West today has been the subject of many scholarly studies and dissertations, and of a full-scale biography. His influence on a later generation of American writers–including not only many younger Jewish novelists but also the Black Humorists of the sixties and such "grotesque" novelists as Flannery O'Connor and John Hawkes–has been remarkable.

In "Nathanael West: A Portrait," S. J. Perelman has described West's physical appearance memorably–"his mouth, a jagged wound etched against the unforgettable blankness of his face"; and he refers to him as a tall man with a stature of only "three inches."[20] The paradox of his being a tall man with a height of only three inches captures well the theme of thwarted identity in West's work, as well as his attraction to dwarfs, freaks, and deformed characters, who, in his view, are symptomatic of man's condition. Perhaps no writer of the thirties was so thoroughly pessimistic as West. No sense of community exists in his fiction, and institutional life and all the communal legacies of the past are voided. Most of all, there is no sense or possibility of love in his novels. Love is reduced always to sexuality–a blind, irrational combat between people, with hostility and violence at its core. Life is envisioned by West nihilistically as an arena of appalling cruelty, in which individuals are maimed, and are unable to establish human contact with others or to transcend their condition through spiritual aspiration. The comedy of their suffering in a world deprived of meaning is the stamp that West has left unforgettably on modern writing.

2

The Dream Life of Balso Snell:
West's Theater of the Unconscious

A tightly written novel of slightly less than sixty pages, darkly shaded by what André Breton called "humour noir,"[1] *Balso Snell* begins with its hero among the ruins of ancient civilization. Treading the tall grass that has grown up around the city of Troy, he encounters the Trojan horse and, in a startling conceit, enters its anus. The interior of the large artifact turns out to be only too physical, and Balso is plunged into a grotesquely unfamiliar world. Like Swift's Gulliver, he has to adjust to a new sense of proportion and perspective, which both reveals and mocks his humanity. As soon as Balso enters the "mystic portal," he notices graffiti carved on the anal lining, a heart pierced by an arrow, with the initial beside it of the Emperor Nero, an inscription that makes the idea of "love" seem dubious.

A minor poet, Balso invokes his muse to steady his nerves, and enters into the "gloom" of the lower intestine, where he encounters a man with the word "Tours" embroidered on his cap. The Jewish guide speaks of his people as "the heirs of Greece and Rome," and seeks to impress on Balso that they represent a culture superior in every respect to the materialistic one Balso belongs to. Balso immediately contests his claims, telling him that the Hebraic tradition ends with sexually predatory Jewish women, and deflates the guide's claims of spirituality further by quoting from C. M. Doughty that the "Semites are like a man sitting in a cloaca to the eyes, and whose brows touch heaven." Rejecting the tour guide as his Virgil, Balso hurries away, as if filled with fear.

Along the turning of the intestine, he encounters another man, Maloney the Areopagite, a Christian gentleman naked except for a derby, a figure whose appearance implies that his decorum only thinly conceals his animal nature. Maloney the Areopagite, more particularly, is a Catholic mystic, bent upon suffering as an atonement for his sins—as evidenced by the thorns stuck in his "phallic" derby and his act, when Balso meets him, of "crucifying" himself with thumbtacks. To Balso, Maloney the Areopagite relates an account of a flea named St. Puce, whose biography he is writing. St. Puce had lived under the armpit of Christ, his vermin's existence made sacrosanct (in his eyes) by drawing his sustenance from the divine being. When Christ is martyred, St. Puce martyrs himself, perishing rather than dwell elsewhere. Appalled by the morbidity of Maloney, whose love of intense suffering seems a warped form of sexual gratification, Balso flees. He rejects the whole Christian-Judaic tradition as a form of mythmaking, which is a dodge from the reality of man's sexuality and, by extension, the anarchy that underlies it. He hurries forward toward what is to be an inward journey.

It is at this point that the novel really begins. Balso now encounters a boy named John Gilson, an eighth-grade pupil in PS 185, who cries: "Reality! Reality! If I could only discover the Real." The boy is the precocious author of a *Crime Journal*, which he leaves in the hollow of a tree (as in an episode from myth or fairy tale), and which Balso removes and reads. The "autobiographical" journal of John Raskolnikov Gilson is narrated in the first person by a man of adult years, beginning with his confinement in an insane asylum, and then circling back to the crime that led him there. Like Dostoyevsky's Raskolnikov, the narrator feels oppressed by the material conditions that weigh on him. He dreams of some act of defiance that will liberate his spirit, give him certitude of his own identity. He spends his days in the public library, a haven for those with odd, misshapen lives, and at night returns alone to his New York rooming house, where he becomes obsessed by another tenant, whom he calls the "idiot."

The *Crime Journal*, which forms one of the most vivid sequences in the novel, is both comic and macabre. The "idiot" is a shapeless, porcine man who reeks of stale tobacco and perspiration odors, and is given to constant laughter. The presence of the idiot disturbs the narrator's "balance," and he decides that if he is to have peace he must kill him. He buys a knife, and on a following night enters the idiot's room and cuts his throat. The manner of the murder is curious, since the narrator first disrobes and commits the act in the nude. At the moment of the murder, as he later recalls it, he reflects: "Naked: I felt cold; and I noticed that my genitals were tight and hard, like a dog's, or an archaic Greek statue's. . . . I was aware of a great excitement."

Then, in a strange sequel, he goes to the river, where he disposes of the knife, and experiences the liberation he has sought, but that is not at all what he had expected:

I felt light and free. I felt like a happy girl. I said to myself: 'You feel like a young girl—kittenish, cuney-cutey, darlingey, spring-timey.' I caressed my breasts like a young girl who has suddenly becoming conscious of her body on a hot afternoon. I imitated the measured walk of a girl showing off before a group of boys. In the dark I hugged myself.

On the way back to Broadway I passed some sailors, and felt an overwhelming desire to flirt with them. I went through all the postures of a desperate prostitute; I camped for all I was worth. The sailors looked at me and laughed. Suddenly I heard the sound of footsteps behind me. The steps came close and I felt as though I were melting—all silk and perfumed, pink lace. I died the little death. But the man went past without noticing me. I sat down on the bench and was violently sick.

Earlier in the sequence the narrator had confided that he had always been tormented by the desire to indulge some strange thing "perceptible but indistinct, hidden in the swamps of my mind." The murder was to have shown his contempt for the animalistic world that surrounded and threatened him; yet instead of liberating him, it leads to a comic-grotesque revelation of his latent homosexuality. With his recognition that the "freedom" he seeks from the physical and sexual is merely an illusion, he becomes insane, and is committed to an asylum. The only escape he is able to find from his animal nature is through insanity.

With the end of this sequence, John Raskolnikov Gilson returns to the tree where he had left his manuscript, and announces to Balso that he had written the *Crime Journal* because his English teacher, Miss McGeeney, reads Russian novels, and that he hopes to ingratiate himself with her and to seduce her. To get rid of the strange boy, Balso buys a pamphlet from him, and, as he begins to read it, another dreamlike sequence unfolds. The narrator of the pamphlet, who remains nameless, is deeply troubled by his lack of identity. Learning of the death of Saniette, the young woman with whom the narrator of the pamphlet had lived for two years, he searches himself for "yesterday's emotions," but can feel nothing. He has read so much, been immersed to such an extent in literature, that there is nothing within him that he can be sure is real. In recounting his misalliance with Saniette, an optimist (whose name suggests "sanitary" or "sane"), while he is the deepest of pessimists, he explains that the absence of the "natural" in him drives him ever further toward a studied cleverness as a means of compelling her admiration. His wholly artificial life makes him wish that he could escape into insanity, and at one point he imagines his revenge on art and culture. "Some day," he remarks, "I shall obtain my revenge by writing a play for one of their art theatres. . . . At the end of the play, the ceiling of the theatre will be made to open and cover the audience with tons of loose excrement." The narrators of John Gilson's manuscripts are both self-entrapped figures: one is morbidly conscious of animality, the other of an unfulfilling rationality, and they cannot free themselves of their obsessions.

As Balso finishes reading the pamphlet narrator's account of his sterile life, with the effect of a camera cut, he finds himself suddenly before a fountain in which a naked young girl is washing her "hidden charms." He rushes to embrace her, but as he does she turns into a middle-aged woman dressed in a "mannish" suit and wearing hornrimmed spectacles. She is Miss McGeeney, a school teacher engaged in writing a biography of Samuel Perkins, who had written a biography of E. F. Fitzgerald, the author of a life of Hobson, who had written a biography of Boswell, the biographer of Johnson. Miss McGeeney begins to discourse on Perkins—until Balso punches her brutally in the stomach and then throws her into the fountain. Seeking relief from what he has experienced, Balso hurries along the intestine to discover a sidewalk café built into its lining. Here, at a table, he falls asleep and has a dream. In his dream regression he is in the lobby of Carnegie Hall, which is crowded with young women who are hunchbacks and who find solace in music. Balso finds them all "beautifully" deformed, especially one, Janey Davenport, who has a hydrocephalic forehead and one-hundred-and-forty-four teeth in rows of four. Balso escorts Janey to her house, where he crudely attempts to seduce her in the hallway. She protests, and, far from giving in to him, asks him to come to her aid by killing Beagle

Darwin, her lover who has jilted her after leaving her with child (carried in the hump on her back). She produces two letters written to her by Beagle, advising her not to follow him to Paris.

The letters begin "Dear Janey," but are not related as letters. Instead, they become little dramas of Beagle's consciousness in which Janey is an actor. In his musings Janey is in Paris; she is pregnant, miserable, and lonely. She seeks "love," to which Darwin, a man made as unreal by his immersion in art as the pamphlet narrator, cannot respond. At one point in his musings, Janey appears to commit suicide by jumping from a window to the street below, just as Beagle himself is approaching. Discovering her body, he retires to a café to ponder what his "reaction" ought to be. Then Janey is present again at the window, and the reader follows the train of her thoughts—a parody of the American girl pleading the cause of love, and conscious of what her mother would think if she knew she had been made pregnant and abandoned in Paris. Suddenly, *accidentally*, Janey loses her footing and falls to her "suicide's" death.

As she falls, Balso awakens from his dream to find himself in the café with Miss McGeeney who, quite suddenly, is metamorphosed into Mary McGeeney, his childhood sweetheart. Balso then takes Mary McGeeney out to a thick clump of bushes behind the café where, comically, she lies on her back with her hands behind her head and her knees spread wide apart. In this parody of sexual love, Mary protests like a good girl, while Balso pleads the case for the satisfaction of their natural desires, summoning up the fleeting sense of time of the Cavalier poets and their demand for passional fulfillment. As the act is engaged in, Balso's body becomes the passive instrument of tremendous biological forces, captured in the imagery of an invincible army. "His body screamed and shouted as it marched and uncoiled," West remarks, "then, with one heaving shout of triumph, it fell back quiet. The army that a moment before had been thundering in his body retreated slowly—victorious, relieved." Balso, at the end, is portrayed comically as the dupe of his own body, and seems the reverse of being powerful and self-asserting. His orgasm is meaningless, and is made all the more so by being experienced only in a wet dream. Worst of all, rather than having grasped the phantom of reality, of having achieved communion with another person, he is alone and pathetic. The novel ends with the sense of Balso's inability to enter life, to find a way out of his consciousness of fragmentation and futility.

Unusual and unique a conception as *Balso Snell* is, it has behind it a large number of shaping influences. Its initial conception, Randall Reid has argued, was inspired by James Branch Cabell's *Jurgen*.[2] Both Jurgen and Balso are poets who begin fantastic journeys by entering a dark cave, and encounter figures representative of the religious and mythic heritage of Western culture. Jurgen throughout, and Balso at certain points, are amorous questers who find that all things end in sex, and that sex ends in disillusionment. In a famous passage of Cabell's novel, Jurgen embraces the lost love of his youth, Dorothy, only to find her suddenly transformed into a middle-aged woman; and Balso has a similar disillusioning experience when he embraces the fountain nymph to find her suddenly changed into the austere, middle-aged Miss McGeeney. Both novels have the form of a search for understanding in a strangely unfamiliar world, which reveals at last that life is irrational and that its meaning cannot be grasped.

But other influences can be noticed in the style of the work. Pound and Eliot, the experimental techniques of the magazine *transition*, and the whole tradition of modernism are reflected in West's concise, allusive, and oblique method. Eliot's *The Waste Land* comes to mind

particularly in West's vision of a fragmented contemporary world of spiritual isolation. Dostoyevsky is prominent in the work, not only in the section of John Raskolnikov Gilson's *Crime Journal* but also in the theme of the
"underground man" who, divided within himself, can
achieve no integration of personality and is doomed to
isolation and inner suffering. West's wide reading in
French literature can also be noticed. Gide's *acte gratuit*,
for example, is intimated in the murder of the "idiot" as a
declaration of freedom; and Baudelaire's poem "Somewhere Out of This World," about the hopelessness of
escape from the oppressive burden of life, is alluded to
specifically. Writers from Flaubert to Huysmans enter
into the novel to emphasize the thwarting of the idealist
by the material world, which West calls the "Mundane
Millstone."

The Dadaists and surrealists are also visible in the
background of the novel. It is the Dadaists who license
West to portray society and cultural nihilism as a fraud.
Balso does not write a manifesto, like Tristan Tzara, but
the pamphlet narrator's imagined revenge upon art, the
releasing of tons of excrement upon the theater audience,
is worthy of the Dadaists. In letters West denied that he
was a surrealist, as in any consistent way he was not, but
he was clearly affected by them in *Balso Snell*. Their
concern with the unconscious, and use of startling dis-
junctions are central to West's novel. In the surrealist
paintings of Picasso and Max Ernst, which West knew
particularly well, the human body is often distorted into
monstrous forms; and West's Janey Davenport, the
hunchback with over a hundred teeth, is a figure from a
dreamlike canvas. One of the characteristic techniques of
the surrealists was the intensely focused, "irrational"
image, and at certain points West draws on this technique.
He writes in surrealist imagery of houses that "are pro-
tuberances on the skin of the streets—warts, tumors, pim-

ples, corns, nipples, sebaceous cysts, hard and soft
chancres," and of "the gums of false teeth, red as the signs
imploring you to enter the game plots lit by iron flowers."

An important distinction between West and the surrealists is that he gives no sense whatever of believing in a
transcendent reality, which the surrealists felt could be
uncovered through the unconscious. Despite the
framework of the unconscious, it is the physical and
material world in which West's characters are mired, and
they are permitted no higher awakenings. West's presentation of his characters through the unconscious is indebted in many respects to Freud, whom West had read,
and whom he called the "modern Bullfinch." Balso's
dream is haunted, damply, by sex, and by sexual fears,
and the characters who people it are unable to find any
satisfactory way out of the dilemma created by their sexuality. Beagle Darwin, whose name is drawn from Darwin's *Voyage of the Beagle*, in which the theory of evolution is put forward, is trapped in the natural world, so
that, less virile than other masculine competitors for the
female, he is forced to develop his intellectual-creative
powers to attract a mate. The enlargement of his artful-
ness, as a means of sexual adaptation, leads, however, to
stultification, to his estrangement from his own body and
from life itself. The lonely, bookish existence of Miss
McGeeney, four times removed from Boswell, and five
times from Dr. Johnson, is symbolic of an attempted
compensation for sexual deprivation, and it gives her
nothing to cling to except a mirage of importance as a
"writer."

West's framing device of the unconscious was also
clearly influenced by James Joyce. Portions of *Finnegans
Wake*,[3] related wholly through the unconscious, had
been published by the time *Balso Snell* was written, and it
is known that West had read and discussed them. He was

also familiar with *Ulysses*, which *Balso Snell* resembles in its having the form of a journey through chaos in a search for the meaning of reality. Both works have Homeric parallels–*Ulysses* elaborately, and *Balso* in the framing device of the Trojan horse–and are comic studies of man's alienation. Joyce's Leopold Bloom is a deracinated Jew in Dublin, while West's Balso is an American of the early thirties who has had some contact with New York and Paris, but belongs nowhere at all. Their experience is dramatized through their interior lives with dreamlike effect. The "Night Town" scene in *Ulysses*, a fantasia of the unconscious, provides West's novel with its form. I. J. Kapstein, an undergraduate friend of West's and later professor of English at Brown,[4] has even called the "Night Town" section "the major influence" on *Balso Snell*.

Joyce's elaborate use of parody also informs West's novel, which contains innumerable instances of parody, including parodies of Joyce himself. At the beginning, when Balso is about to enter the lower intestine of the horse, he invokes his muse, like Stephen Dedalus at the end of *A Portrait of the Artist as a Young Man*. Somewhat self-importantly, Dedalus prepares to forge in the "smithy" of his soul the uncreated conscience of his race, and calls upon his mythic "father" to "stand me now as ever in good stead." In West's version, Balso exclaims: "O Beer! O Meyerbeer! O Bach! O Offenbach! Stand me now as ever in good stead." In a brilliant parody at the end, Mary McGeeney surrenders to passion with Balso in a murmurous swoon reminiscent of Molly Bloom's "yes, yes, I said, yes" acceptance of nature. In her "acceptance," Mary sighs: "Moompitcher, yaah. O I never hoped to know the passion, the sensuality hidden within you–yes, yes. Drag me down into the mire, drag. Yes. And with your hair the lust from my eyes brush. Yes . . . Yes . . . Ooo! Ah!" Her preposterous bathos is matched by the futility of Balso's orgasm, which signals his final defeat.

Balso Snell has the patterning of the "high quest," the noble adventure, yet has as its hero, if he can be called that, a man who lacks dimension and size, and who, in particular, seems sexually insecure and inadequate. Christ is frequently alluded to, evoked, called upon, but he appears in the Maloney the Areopagite section in a manner that emphasizes his merely physical nature—and grotesquely at that, since his flesh is infested with vermin. In West's profane satire of the Communion, St. Puce drinks the blood and eats the flesh of the Savior, but he is merely a flea and, in addition, is an illusionist who imagines his mean existence as a holy life. With a similar strategy of deflation, West uses Christ to comment on the banality of man's quest for sublimity. "At your birth," the pamphlet narrator comments, "instead of the Three Kings, the Dove, the Star of Bethlehem, there was only old Doctor Hausenschweitz who wore rubber gloves and carried a towel over his arm like a waiter."

In an early section of the novel one of the dominant images West uses is that of the circle, meant to suggest perfection and divinity. But in Balso's opening "song," the circle is illustrated not only by the "perfect circles" painted by Giotto and the navel of "Mary Our Mother," but also by the round holes in Christ's feet from "the Jew-driven nails," which makes the quest for divinity end in worldly crucifixion. The circle imagery comes to suggest a painful self-enclosure, with aspiration followed by failure in an endlessly repeated cycle. The failure to break free of the circle in which the individual is psychically bound prefigures the ending in which Balso is doomed to repeat a pattern of frustration, imposed upon him by his involvement with natural and bodily processes.

The quest for sublimity and its frustration is also implicated in the philosophical issues that are at various times raised. Monism is accepted as a "given" by the tour guide, but Balso is conscious of the pluralistic nature of existence. If God is pervasive, why are there such particular *feet*, and why are these feet so repelling? That the spiritual and physical exist on planes that cannot be joined is implied in Balso's taunt to the tour guide that he arrange in advance, by "wireless," to have two parallel lines meet. The hopelessness of the wireless communication between spirit and world has a Kafkaesque quality, and is characteristic of the sense of life in *Balso Snell* as an arena of radical disjunction and incoherence.

One of West's stranger satires of the attempt to find order in life through the medium of art is occasioned by Miss McGeeney's discourse on Samuel Perkins, the subject of her curious biography *Samuel Perkins: Smeller*. Perkins's face, it seems, was dominated by his nose. Deaf and almost blind, he developed an abnormal acuteness to odor, to the point that he believed he could find unity and system in nature. This parody of Rimbaud's theory of synesthesia (and of Huysmans's epicurean hero Des Esseintes) involves the reader in endless instances of disagreeable odors, particularly excremental ones. Writing of West's turn of mind as a high-school student, Jay Martin has remarked that "he showed . . . a striking preoccupation with the human body, particularly with its odors, its orifices, its corruptibility and diseases, with parasites that feed on the human body." These preoccupations are all present, if not pervasive, in *Balso Snell*.

The hero's name, as Randall Reid has pointed out, is meant to suggest "balls' smell," and his B. S. initials carry the implication of animal ordure. Together with excremental imagery, one finds an overriding and morbid concern with physical blemishes, disfigurement, and deformities. The *Crime Journal* narrator lives in a rooming house filled with stifling odors, and lies in his room for hours "overpowered by the heat, odor, and nastiness of

I." The idiot, who occupies a room on the same floor, has an enlarged Adam's apple that, in a typically grotesque Westian image, "looked as though it might be a soft tumor in his throat"; and he is associated specifically with excrement, making a noise when he swallows that sounds like a "toilet being flushed." In a passage obviously intended to shock the reader, John Raskolnikov Gilson, before beginning the *Crime Journal*, which is his attempt to find transcendence through art, smells his "moistened forefinger," which he has, presumably, put into his rectum.

West's attack on art, which purports to have a "meaning-making" function, to be able to impose order on life's chaos, is one of the most striking features of the novel. Primarily, West is concerned with writers, many of whom appear by name – Nietzsche, Bergson, Daudet, Huysmans, Cabell, DeSade, Baudelaire, and William James, to mention only some. Often they are parodied, with their own words used against them. George Moore had remarked that "Art is not nature, but rather nature digested," which leads to the observation in the work that art is "a sublime excrement." Similarly, West parodies Lawrence's phoenix symbol of the artist's self-regeneration by having Balso recall the "Phoenix Excrementi," a people he has imagined who "eat themselves, digest themselves, and give birth to themselves by evacuating their bowels." The pretension of art to know what reality is, and thus to raise man above the disorder of his condition, is rejected as a deception and illusion.

The Trojan horse itself, which frames the novel's action and is always in the reader's mind, had been given treacherously by the Greeks to the Trojans, and was a work of art intended to deceive. The characters who are encountered in its intestinal tract are all involved, in one form or another, in a charade of identity, and many of them are neurotic artists, or more specifically writers.

Balso is himself a poet, and his dream is filled with writer-characters who, like the characters in Pirandello's plays, are in search of reality. John Raskolnikov Gilson is a precocious child author (a parody of Rimbaud and other precocious "seer"-poets of the nineteenth century); the sexually thwarted Miss McGeeney writes on academic subjects; and Maloney the Areopagite, whose saintly aspirations disguise his sexual masochism, has written a hagiography of St. Puce, who, in turn, has attempted to make his vermin's life meaningful by writing a book, *A Geography of Our Lord*. They are said to be "writers in search of an audience," but it might better be said of them that they are in search of themselves, for they all have merely phantom existences.

The impression they give of estrangement has been achieved through a variety of effects that distance them from life. The dream context itself makes them seem unreal, since they are permitted no life except insofar as they participate in Balso's drama of the unconscious that is filled with shifting appearances and unsettling contradictions. The writer-characters, furthermore, are unreliable. Janey Davenport, the "Lepi," as West calls her, is an apparently "normal" girl (rather than the hunchback she had been when she is first seen) in Beagle Darwin's letters—which turn out to have been written not by him but by Miss McGeeney. John Raskolnikov Gilson allows Balso to read what he has written, but warns that what he wrote may not necessarily be true, and was, in any case, written with ulterior motives. Most of all, he is a child still in his puberty, and cannot be an authority on the adult experience he details. Faced with so many contradictions, so many characters who deceive themselves and others, the reader is swayed to regard West's characters as refugees from life rather than as real participants in it.

The sense of the characters' estrangement is increased by the absence of any meaningful communication be-

tween them. In the opening section, Balso talks at cross
purposes with the tour guide and Maloney the Areopagite, and in the later sections he meets but never establishes contact with the other characters. Men and women,
particularly, are cut off from one another as they attempt
to meet across the barrier of sexuality. West's women are
all distinctly limited as human beings and are painfully
maimed. Miss McGeeney's life is a bookish ostracism,
while Janey Davenport, who clings to a movie version of
love, is a freak. West's men are more intellectual than his
women, but their introspective natures merely act to keep
them from emotional commitment. The *Crime Journal*
narrator, the pamphlet narrator, and Beagle Darwin can
find no sense of fulfillment and are themselves "unreal."
The result is that West's characters are committed to their
own solitude, can brush against one another but never
enter into understanding or intimacy. As *Balso Snell*
progresses, it takes on the aspect of a theater of isolated
voices, of individuals who cannot find their way into
life

One of the principal aesthetic strategies West adopts
in the work, indeed, is his use of "theater" as theme and
technique. The novel itself has a dramatic structure, with
a prologue section in which the tour guide and Maloney
the Areopagite appear, followed by a series of sharply
visualized "scenes," and concluding with a love scene between Balso and Mary McGeeney that is strongly climactic in effect. More importantly, the characters within the
work are all role players, often in a stylized way that
emphasizes their involvement in illusion. The tour guide
is bound by the edicts of the Hebraic tradition he speaks
for, and Maloney the Areopagite is a self-conscious
spokesman for the Christian tradition, even going so far
as to posture in the attitude of the martyred Christ. He is
"theatrical" in his adoption of an identity, is all pose and
no self; and like him, the other characters in Balso's thea-

ter of the unconscious pretend to identities that seem dubious or delusionary.

In the opening, when Balso discovers a heart pierced by an arrow, together with the initial *N*, on the portal of the anus, West refers to Nero as "the actor-emperor," with the implication that he has deceived himself through self-dramatization, his cruel passions having nothing to do with "love." Christ on the cross is also evoked with a mocking theatricality. "The hot sun of Calvary," West writes, "burnt the flesh beneath Christ's upturned arm, making the petal-like skin shrivel until it looked like the much shaven armpit of an old actress." As an "old actress," Christ is implied to be playing a part, to be "feminine" in the passive suffering he cultivates while all look on. The "love" he dramatizes is undermined by the suggestion of disguised sexual masochism.

The *Crime Journal* narrator plays a role that has already been established for him by Dostoyevsky, so that he does not so much create his life as reenact a role. His experience makes a distinct "drama," framed by the asylum, to which he will later be committed, and the theatrical rooming house in the West Forties, the theater district where he lives miserably. The idiot, who lives nearby in the same building, is compared to a pig, and the narrator slashes his throat with a knife in a melodramatic murder. The theatrical frame reinforces the sense of the *Crime Journal* narrator as an illusionist. What before long becomes apparent is that the idiot is the narrator's double, his animal self that he cannot destroy and from which he cannot escape. If in the theater of his mind he envisions radical freedom, he becomes in the end an illustration of West's remark that "life is a prison without bars."

The pamphlet narrator, who has the center stage as a monologuist in Gilson's second tale, is similarly self-imprisoned. Analyzing why it is that he dislikes Saniette, he declares: "a large part of it consists of [the] antipathy felt by the performer for his audience. My relations with Saniette were exactly those of performer and audience. . . . I have forgotten the time when I could look back at an affair with a woman and remember anything but a series of theatrical poses—poses that I assumed, no matter how aware I was of their ridiculousness." Unable to compete with better looking or more virile men, he is compelled to stun Saniette into an admiration of his mind, something that he is forced to repeat endlessly, even while conscious that he is a sham, since what drives him to "act" as he does is the rudimentary "Desire to Procreate."

Beagle Darwin, who is emotionally empty and can only pretend to that which he can no longer feel, is compared to "an old actor mumbling Macbeth as he fumbles in the garbage can outside the theatre of his past triumphs." More pointedly, he is compared to Hamlet, even calling himself Beagle Hamlet Darwin. Sickly introspective, he is an outsider to life. Nothing happens to him, he can only imagine it happening, in his putative letters, to someone else, specifically to Janey Davenport. In his imagination, she plays the role, whether she wishes to or not, of the lovelorn suicide in Paris. It is a self-dramatizing role, undercut by its triteness and by Beagle's failure of response. In the sidewalk café to which he retires to reflect, he imagines the announcement of her death to him in the café in the form of classical drama. Euripidean messengers enter with the tragic news, and a chorus is introduced to add to the heightened effect of the scene; but such overheightening merely adds to the sense that Janey's death is an empty joke, as empty as Beagle's own life.

In an extension of this theater theme, West at times imagines his characters as "clowns" who perform on a stage. The *Crime Journal* narrator cannot bear the sight of the idiot, who has the appearance of a clown, a man "whose head was all face—a face without side, back or top, like a mask." He wears a mask because he has no identity, and he laughs incessantly. Since he is the narrator's *doppelgänger*, the narrator too must be understood as a clown, a fool without a knowable self. Moreover, the motif of the clown is reiterated incrementally in the course of the work. The pamphlet narrator, in discussing his relationship to Saniette, remarks: "I watched carefully to see how she received my performance, whether with a smile or a tear. Though I exhibited myself as a clown, I wanted no mistake to be made; I was a tragic clown." He is comparable, perhaps, to one of Picasso's clowns, who are alone in an empty universe.

The clown motif is expressed most fully, however, in the section devoted to Beagle Darwin, who sums up life in the following way:

A throe of pain, a spasm of volupty: then a gasping for breath, and the comedy is over, the song is ended, ring down the curtain, the clown is dead. . . . The clown is dead, the curtain is down. And when I say clown, I mean you. After all, aren't we all . . . aren't we all clowns? . . . Life *is* a stage; and *we* are clowns.

Beagle even imagines himself as a clown performing on stage, pretending to unfelt emotions, while "the clowns down front are laughing." His finale is given the form of an irreligious burlesque. "After building up his tear-jerker routine for a repeat," West writes, "he blacked out and went into his juggling for the curtain. He climaxed the finale by keeping in the air an Ivory Tower, a Still White Bird, the Holy Grain, the Nails, the Scourge, the Thorns, and a piece of the True Cross." The high quest here is reduced to vaudeville.[5]

As it happens, West was strongly attracted to vaudeville as a child in New York. He went to see many vaudeville performances, and continued to do so in his adult years.

To friends he insisted that vaudeville was classical in form, and compared it to Greek comedy. If one looks at *Balso Snell* closely, versions of vaudeville and burlesque can be seen at many points. Balso's skirmishing with the tour guide and Maloney the Areopagite is, at a rudimentary level, buffoonery. Janey Davenport's fall to her death in Paris is slapstick. Balso is the Everyman figure of the novel, and derives in a sense from Bunyan, but the final comic deflation of him reveals his affinities with the vaudeville circuit, with the little man who prompts guffaws by being quashed on stage. The theater and clown motifs give West an affinity, indeed, with Beckett and the Theater of the Absurd. Beckett, too, was unusually conscious of vaudeville, and incorporated it into his plays of the modern Everyman's search for meaning in life. Like Balso, Beckett's searchers are foiled—are pitiful clowns, stunted individuals who are quintessentially alone.

Despite the universality of its themes, however, *Balso Snell* gives the impression of a very deep personal frustration in West himself. It is evident particularly in his obsession with sexual thwarting and stunting. West's attitude toward women, who fare very badly in the novel's phobic dream, is striking in the hostility it reveals. The female is associated with disagreeable smells, with ulcerations and herniated intestines and venereal disease. Nipples are included in the same context as pimples and cysts, and the vagina is depicted as an unlovely garden of "sticky . . . mucous membrane." In one passage, women craving sex are "clad in the silk tights of pleasure, oiled with fish slime." Janey Davenport's one-hundred-and-forty-four teeth give her a threateningly voracious quality.

In whatever form they appear in *Balso Snell*, women have a threatening aspect and elicit high levels of anger and violence. When Balso spies a naked girl in the fountain, he grabs her and sticks his tongue into her mouth as if his tongue were an assaultive weapon; and in another passage, a vagina is "slit" as with a cruelly sharp knife. Typically, West's women are humiliated and assaulted. Miss McGeeney is struck a violent blow to the abdomen by Balso, who would actually have preferred "breaking her jaw in." Saniette is beaten at least twice by the pamphlet narrator, and is punished further by dying.

Other aspects of the sexuality in the novel raise questions about West's psychology. His attitude toward mothers tends to be hostile when it appears, sometimes in the form of women like Janey Davenport, who seek to dominate men as mother figures; and these mother surrogates suggest a ripe Oedipal drama. Who, after all, is John Raskolnikov Gilson, the schoolboy who reads Russian literature, particularly Dostoyevsky, at a precocious age, while harboring a sexual attraction to a mature woman close to him? If he is not West, he has at least a Westian ambivalence. At the end Balso has sexual relations with Mary McGeeney, his childhood sweetheart, but partly because of earlier allusions to "Mary Our Mother," she may also be Balso's mother, triumphant in her seduction of him—a climactic moment which reveals that he cannot "grow up," liberate himself into larger life.

Even if West is implying that Balso's Oedipal situation is Everyman's, as part of his enclosure in a cycle of frustration, other questions remain. The question, for example, of homoeroticism, which accompanies the attraction to but repulsion from women, remains. The Trojan horse is penetrated anally by Balso at the beginning, and since the implications of the horse are presumably masculine,[6] as they are always in D. H. Lawrence, the act is tantamount to sodomy. This implication is heightened by West's wicked and obviously cherished allusion to the philosopher-saint Appolonius of Tyana, who keeps a snake in his anus—another instance of phallic-anal penetration. Moreover, one of the most strikingly rendered sexual scenes in the novel occurs between two men, the *Crime Journal* narrator and the idiot, a scene that leads to the narrator's disturbing recognition of his latent homosexuality.

West's theme that life consists of irreducible sexual frustration often makes one wonder if West is not commenting on himself, just as his concern with the thwarted "writer" figure, who cannot relate directly to life, reflects West's own situation as a young man writing his first novel. *Balso Snell*, indeed, is a highly self-conscious work, in which West is sometimes guilty of admiring his own cleverness. One notes in it, too, lapses of authorial control, particularly in those passages in which West's humor seems forced. Commenting on the studied nature of the novel, Randall Reid has remarked: "Only when [West] abandons physical buffoonery for verbal parody—as in Miss McGeeney's seduction responses—does his performance become assured and hilarious. And even then his success depends upon the cool precision of each phrase, not on an exuberant display of energy."[7] One of the best comments on the limitations of the novel is that of Kingsley Widmer, who notes that it lacks a context, which would give West's parodies a sense of reality.[8] Lacking such a context in the real world, the novel has the attenuated quality of its characters.

But *Balso Snell* ought not to be simply dismissed as an exercise. It is, in its way, a highly styled work, which reveals a good deal of intelligence and aesthetic sophistication. Especially evident in the novel is West's gift for miniaturization, as can be seen in the *Crime Journal* when John Gilson's mother visits him at the asylum. "My mother rolls on the hospital floor," Gilson writes, "and cries: 'John darling . . . John sweetheart.' Her hat falls over her face. She clutches a bag of oranges." In this cameo moment one recognizes how much West's strength, even in the early stages of his career, lies in his use of the concentrated, arresting image. The novel also forecasts West's later themes—the quest, the encounter with illusion in an empty world, the drama of sexual ambivalence involving violence upon women, and the fragmentation of identity.

Present in *Balso Snell*, too, are intimations of the Christ theme, which appears more prominently, and with a sharper focusing, in *Miss Lonelyhearts*. Saniette, the simple-minded optimist who cannot understand her more complicated lover, will be reimagined as Miss Lonelyhearts's girl friend Betty. The mocking tone Balso adopts late in the work also predicts another of the novel's characters. After reading the letters of Beagle Darwin that Miss McGeeney claims to have written, Balso tells her with brutal sarcasm: "A stormy wind blows through your pages, sweeping the reader breathless. . . . It is a drama of passion that has all the appeal of wild living and the open road. . . . There's magic in its pages, and warm sympathy for an alien race." This is the assaultively ironic voice of Shrike as it is about to be created. Only two years separate *Balso Snell* from the publication of *Miss Lonelyhearts*, but it is a time of remarkable growth for West as a novelist. In his second time out, the "bad boy" who wrote *Balso Snell* will actually produce a work of genius.

3

Miss Lonelyhearts:
The Absurd Center of the Dead World

West's initial conception of *Miss Lonelyhearts* grew out of an incident that occurred in March 1929. S. J. Perelman invited West to join him at Siegel's restaurant in Greenwich Village where he was to have dinner with a newspaperwoman who wrote a lovelorn column for the *Brooklyn Eagle* under the name "Susan Chester." At the restaurant, "Susan Chester" read aloud some of the letters from her readers, thinking that Perelman might be able to put them to comic use. He did not find them especially promising as material for satire, but West was moved, and intrigued, by them; and they became the starting point for his novel,[1] which evolved slowly, passing through six different drafts, before being completed in December 1932.

Although the earliest drafts of the novel have not survived, the later stages of West's revision can be glimpsed in five next-to-final chapter drafts published in *Contact* and *Contempo* magazines in 1932,[2] a year before the publication of the work. They reveal that even in this later stage of composition he was still attempting to resolve the problem of how best to present the protagonist. In the February 1932 issue of *Contact*, the third-person protagonist is called Thomas Matlock, but in the May issue West's narration shifts to the first person, and in the October issue back again to the third. Clearly, a first-person narration would have diminished the author's ironic judgment of the hero—and proved unmanageable at the end, when he is killed. Clearly, too, while using the name homas Matlock in the first segment, West had decided to dispense with a name for him at all, other than Miss Lonelyhearts, as the work progressed, thus achieving adtional irony—a relentless challenging of the hero's identity.

Another conspicuous feature of West's revision is that in the earlier version Miss Lonelyhearts and Shrike were not as absolutely antithetical as they later became. The earlier Miss Lonelyhearts indulged in moments of self-mockery that, in revision, were rewritten as a mockery of him by Shrike. Indeed, a whole sequence in the first draft of "Miss Lonelyhearts in the Dismal Swamp," in which Miss Lonelyhearts ponders, only to reject as fruitless, avenues of escape from his despair (the South Seas, the arts, the farm), was later given to Shrike. Moreover, this lengthy, rather lushly parodic passage is out of key stylistically with the rest of the work. In rewriting, West reduced the length and tone of the passage considerably, making it suitable to be spoken mockingly by Shrike as Miss Lonelyhearts's alter ego.

West's revisions almost always work toward greater cohesiveness and concreteness, as can be seen in the opening sentences in the February 1932 and April 1933 versions:

February 1932	*April 1933*
Thomas Matlock, the Miss Lonelyhearts of the New York Evening Hawk (Are you in trouble? Do you need advice? Write to Miss Lonelyhearts and she will help you) decided to walk from the Hawk Building across the park to Delehanty's speakeasy.	The Miss Lonelyhearts of the New York Herald *Post-Dispatch* (Are-you-in-trouble?-Do-you-need-advice?-write-to-Miss-Lonelyhearts-and-she-will-help-you) sat at his desk and stared at a piece of white cardboard.

Not only has the actual name for Miss Lonelyhearts been removed, but the name of the newspaper has also been changed for the sake of greater realism; and the lines lead directly to the blasphemous prayer Shrike has had printed, bringing the reader immediately to the heart of the conflict within the hero. Elsewhere, in the first-person draft, the hero attempts to explain himself to the reader: "Don't misunderstand me. My Christ has nothing to do with love. Even before I became Miss Lonelyhearts, my world was moribund. I lived on a deserted stairway of ornate machinery. I wrote my first love letters on a typewriter. . . . I turned to Christ as the most familiar and natural of excitants. I wanted him to destroy this hypnosis. He alone could make the rock of sensation bleed and the stick of thought flower." This explanatory passage was deleted in revision, allowing the reader more dramatically to grasp Miss Lonelyhearts's mental state through understatement.

The revisions also show West confronting and over-coming problems of diffuseness. In the early draft of the opening chapter Miss Lonelyhearts prepares to go to Delehanty's, and on the way pauses to rest for a moment on a bench in the small park. But here he decides against going to the speakeasy after all, returns home, goes to bed, and reads Father Zosima's sermon in *The Brothers Karamazov*, after which he falls asleep and has a dream in which he and two other college friends, on a drinking spree, decide to sacrifice a lamb in a quasi-religious cere-mony, a botched attempt that turns into sordid cruelty. In revision, Miss Lonelyhearts, in his office, is reading the letters from Sick-of-it-all and Desperate when Shrike appears, and their first confrontation concludes the chap-ter dramatically. In the second chapter he not only pre-pares to go but does go to Delehanty's, where he meets Shrike and Miss Farkis, a strikingly self-contained "scene." Only in the next chapter does Miss Lonelyhearts return home to read the Father Zosima passage and have the dream. With far greater concentration of effect, West finds the proper place for the lamb incident, which dominates the chapter in which it appears.

Other revisions reveal West's attention to nuance. In the early part, for example, the mirror on the wall of Miss Lonelyhearts's room, an emblem of his introspection, is removed. The sacrifice of the lamb scene is bathed in blood in the early draft ("A thick stream of blood pumped over their heads and clothes"), but is muted in the later one. A dream in which he appears as a child in a flannel nightgown, with his head bent in prayer on the knees of the mother he innocently "loved," a scene which precedes his later rage over the loss of love, is removed as being too explicit. In the early draft, the letter from Broad Shoulders contains more pedestrian details and is less powerful than the letter as it appears in the final version, an indication of how carefully West weighed every word, how he built up effects in revision as well as toned them down.

All the magazine-draft chapters contain lines and passages that were refined upon in the book version. In certain cases names were changed. Fay Doyle's husband was named Martin before becoming Peter, and her daughter Lucy was at first named Mary. In some instances, gross touches were softened. The "clean old man" at the comfort station is said to turn away "to wipe himself with some paper from the roll beside the seat," but in the book version he turns away "to wipe his mouth." In the seduction scene, Fay Doyle "caught [Miss Lonelyhearts's] head and put her tongue into his mouth"—which in the book version becomes, "and kissed him on the mouth." The revisions include scores of minor alterations, all of which contribute to the polish of the final draft. In general, West's tendency is to abbreviate, foreshorten, and to avoid direct statement or explanation; and in this way the novel becomes not only more certain in its tone but also more cryptic and mysterious.

If the revisions reveal West's refinement upon his conception, they do not, of course, explain the conception. West himself has commented on the composition of *Miss Lonelyhearts* in "Some Notes on Miss L.," published in *Contempo* magazine in 1933;[3] but it is difficult to know how seriously to take what he says. He explains that *Miss Lonelyhearts* "became the portrait of a priest of our time who has a religious experience. His case is classical and is built on all the cases in James' *Varieties of Religious Experience* and Starbuck's *Psychology of Religion*. The psychology is theirs not mine. The imagery is mine." He also remarks that while writing the novel, he conceived of it as a comic strip:

The chapters to be squares in which many things happen through one action. The speeches contained in conventional balloons. I abandoned this idea, but retained some of the comic strip technique: Each chapter instead of going forward in time, also goes backward, forward, up and down in space like a picture. Violent images are used to illustrate commonplace events. Violent acts are left almost bald.[4]

Miss Lonelyhearts does have something of the nature of a comic strip or cartoon. Each chapter is dramatically focused by a single event or brief sequence of events, comparable to the series of pictorial frames of a comic strip. Like the figures in a cartoon, West's characters are stripped down to the sharp outline of a few traits. Pete Doyle is a cripple, his wife is sexually devouring, Betty is simple and unworldly, Shrike is a mocker. They have also been strongly visualized (Miss Lonelyhearts's long, bony "biblical" face, and Pete Doyle's built-up shoe which he drags after him), and West makes frequent use of the tableau. The endings of the chapters, particularly, often use framing tableaux that bring the chapters to visual climaxes. The novel's denouement also has the graphic, pictorial quality of a comic strip ending–Miss Lonelyhearts's fall on the staircase a visual analogue of his fall from the grace he had just imagined.

But if *Miss Lonelyhearts* is a comic strip, it is a distinctly sinister one. A death theme runs through it, evoking a dead world that cannot be brought to life, and the novel ends with death. One of the prominent features of *Miss Lonelyhearts*, as compared to *Balso Snell*, is the manner in which West moves from an indeterminate interior landscape that can be located nowhere in time and space to a concrete social setting of the thirties. Its setting, with the exception of a brief visit to the Connecticut countryside, is New York, which has been created with a harsh stylization that could be compared to the hard-boiled detective fiction of Dashiell Hammett. Hammett, in fact, was West's guest at the Sutton Hotel when *Miss Lonelyhearts* was being written, and he read the novel in an early draft. West, in turn, had read Hammett's detective novels, as well as many of the issues of *Black Mask*, the great magazine forum for hard-boiled detective fiction of the thirties. When *Miss Lonelyhearts* was published, Josephine Herbst called it a "moral detective story"–and it does give the impression of a raw world in which values have disappeared, and in which violence is sudden and frequent. As in Hammett's fiction, the quester figure is alone in what is essentially an irrational world; and curiously, in the early draft, but later removed, Miss Lonelyhearts is even compared to a detective. As he waits in the park for Mrs. Doyle to appear, he examines the sky "like a stupid detective who is searching for a clue to his own exhaustion." A few minutes later, "the detective saw a big woman enter the park and start in his direction." Miss Lonelyhearts is evoked here as a man who searches for clues to the mystery of an absent God, and in his later wanderings he attempts but fails to unravel the mystery.

The hard-boiled aspect of *Miss Lonelyhearts* can be

noticed in chapter 5, which begins in Delehanty's speakeasy as a group of nameless, dimensionless men assault women verbally, particularly women writers who pretend to one aesthetic ideal or another. One of the men tells of a woman writer who was hurt "by beauty," and is taken "into the lots" one night by eight men and gang raped, presumably as a curative for her illusions. Another man relates a story about a female writer who cultivated "hard-boiled stuff," and is assaulted and sexually abused for three days by a group of hardened, low-life men who resent her glamorization of the primitive and physical. Not only is violence recounted by these men in the accents of a calloused dehumanization, it also erupts in fact. Miss Lonelyhearts is struck suddenly in the face at one point, and by the end of the chapter, in another speakeasy, he is hit over the head with a chair. The chapter ends with his loss of consciousness. West's characters, in fact, show very little consciousness of any kind, whether social, aesthetic, or political.

Although *Miss Lonelyhearts* is not a political novel, a criticism of capitalism does enter into it. In *Miss Lonelyhearts*, unlike *Balso Snell*, West is unusually conscious of the life of the masses, of a suffering that he has related to society's complicity in the dehumanization of its members, its trashing of their very dreams. Miss Lonelyhearts's girl friend Betty, who represents the status quo and does not question it, wants him to go to work for an advertising agency, where he will be a manipulator of dreams for commercial ends. As it is, as a newspaper columnist, he offers mere palliatives for suffering, all that his spiritually deadened society can provide its members.

About the role of society in the manipulation of dreams, West is quite explicit. "Men have always," he writes, "fought their misery with dreams. Although dreams were once powerful, they have been made puerile

by the movies, radio and newspapers. Among many be-
trayals this one is the worst." Miss Lonelyhearts often
seems, powerlessly, like a man in a cage. His solitary
room and office at the newspaper are like boxes; and in an
earlier draft the street upon which he looks from his office
window is "walled at both ends." In his office he meditates on life as a desert, a place of inertia, animality, and
violence, which are part of everyday life. His petitioners
for help seem to him to live in little enclosed spaces, surrounded by commercial billboards that serve as remind-
ers of violated values. In such a meaningless world, violence is a logical outcome.

Elsewhere, in a dream sequence, Miss Lonelyhearts is
in the window of a pawnshop, where he attempts to
create order out of the paraphernalia around him. He tries
to assemble stable shapes from the musical instruments,
umbrellas, and derby hats, and eventually forms a large
cross. When the cross becomes too large for the
pawnshop, he moves it, in his imagination, to the shore of
the ocean. But here each wave throws up more debris,
adding to the stock of the cross faster than he can extend
its arms, and he becomes a kind of Sisyphus struggling
with an impossible task. The sequence implies the impos-
sibility of Miss Lonelyhearts's effort to create order out
of chaos; but the pawnshop image is particularly interesting, since it evokes the discarding or destruction of
dreams in a commercial society. When West refers to "the
business of dreams," he implies that human dreams are an
industry for capitalist exploitation. In an early section,
Shrike produces a newspaper clipping about a religious
sect that will hold a "goat and adding machine ritual" for
a man about to be executed in a Colorado prison. The
clipping is of course a parody of American religious sects
that have become "worldly" and incoherent. But it also
suggests that the prisoner, who slew another man in an
argument over a small amount of money, is a "goat," or

scapegoat of the society, in which spiritual reality is no more meaningful than the figures in an adding-machine tally.

Although West does not refer specifically to the Depression, it is an unnamed presence in the novel.[5] When Miss Lonelyhearts returns from his escape vacation in the country, the first thing he notices as he drives into the city are the Bronx slums. It is at this point that he recognizes the hopelessness of his "mission." People wander the streets with "broken hands" and "torn mouths." A man on the verge of death staggers into a movie theater showing a film called *Blonde Beauty*, an escapist sexual fantasy; and a ragged woman with "an enormous goiter" gleefully picks a love-story magazine out of a garbage can. These are the betrayed ones, betrayed by their culture—the spiritually beggared.

West's portrait of Miss Lonelyhearts, however, is less a social than a psychological study, one which is indebted particularly to Dostoyevsky.[6] Dostoyevsky's "underground man" supplies the model for Miss Lonelyhearts's self-division and psychological suffering; and Raskolnikov[7] in *Crime and Punishment* especially prepares for him—in his impulse to play a heroic role for which he is not necessarily qualified, his fevered dreams, isolation within an oppressive society, and obsession. As if to make the Russian analogy unmistakable, West has Goldsmith, an underling of Shrike's, address Miss Lonelyhearts by asking "How now, Dostoievsky?" Dostoyevsky is referred to again when Miss Lonelyhearts withdraws to his room to read *The Brothers Karamazov*, and Father Zosima's sermon is quoted: "Love the animals, love the plants, love everything. If you love everything, you will perceive the divine mystery in things. Once you perceive it, you will begin to comprehend it better every day. And you will come at last to love the whole world with an all-embracing love." It is this vision of an all-embracing love that torments Miss Lonelyhearts with its unattainability, and is part of his "Christ complex."

Miss Lonelyhearts is also similar in a number of essentials to Prince Myshkin, in *The Idiot*, who yearns for a community of Christian love and brotherhood in a society that would seem to deny its possibility absolutely. Alone, in a deeply disillusioning world, Prince Myshkin finds that he can only be misunderstood, and becomes increasingly estranged. In the end his retirement to the Swiss sanitarium indicates the futility of his quest. Like Myshkin, Miss Lonelyhearts is set apart from others by his spiritual aspiration that is out of key with the materialistic world in which he lives, so that he is regarded as a freak and suffers the torment of the misfit. To his friend John Sanford, West boasted that he could rewrite Dostoyevsky "with a pair of shears"; and remarkably he has done just that, reproducing Dostoyevsky in miniature in an American Depression setting.

Miss Lonelyhearts's dreams are inner psychological dramas, like the dreams in Dostoyevsky, but they have also been influenced by Freud and the surrealists. Freudian symbolism is apparent, for example, in the scene in which Miss Lonelyhearts meditates in the little park near a Mexican War obelisk. "He sat staring at [the obelisk] without knowing why," West comments, "until he noticed that it was lengthening in rapid jerks, not as shadows usually lengthen. He grew frightened and looked up quickly at the monument. It seemed red and swollen in the dying sun, as though it were about to spout a load of granite seed." A moment later, his thoughts turn to the desire for sex that he has been suppressing. The scene is not actually a dream but it is something like a dream state, and another dream state occurs when Miss Lonelyhearts drives through the Bronx slums, where "crowds of people moved through the street with a dream-like violence," an image that might have come from a surrealist canvas. In an actual dream late in the novel, West's imagery is oddly reminiscent of a Salvador Dali painting: "A train rolled into a station, where [Miss Lonelyhearts] was a reclining statue holding a stopped clock, a coach rumbled into the yard of an inn where he was sitting over a guitar, cap in hand, shedding the rain with his hump."

Miss Lonelyhearts takes much of its life from West's striking and haunting imagery. It is difficult to say how West learned to use imagery to such effect, but he may well have been influenced by the poetry of the period–by the Imagists, Ezra Pound, and William Carlos Williams, in whose verse the image takes on a luminous life of its own. He was undoubtedly influenced by T. S. Eliot, since the symbolism of *The Waste Land* is apparent in the novel. *The Waste Land* theme is particularly evident in West's depiction of the small, barren park, which ought to be a spiritual oasis in the city but is instead a miniature wasteland–a setting of dessication and blight. Describing the little park, West writes: "The decay that covered the surface of the mottled ground was not the kind in which life generates. Last year, he remembered, May had failed to quicken these soiled fields. It had taken all the brutality of July to torture a few green spikes through the exhausted dirt." In this wasteland park, Miss Lonelyhearts waits for a spring that does not come–until the end, when it brings only death. [8]

Although hardly noted in the past, Fitzgerald's *The Great Gatsby* is also a decided influence on West's novel. [9] Both are classic works of miniaturization that are tragic and comic at once, and end with the death of the heroes, who have been obsessed with an illusion of spiritual transcendence. If *Miss Lonelyhearts* has a cartoon quality, its characters limned in sinister caricature, so does *The Great Gatsby*. Myrtle Wilson, in *The Great Gatsby*,

establishes the type of the cheap, sexual woman, preposterous in her vulgarity, who is reimagined exuberantly by
West in Fay Doyle. Fay has, in fact, the name of another
character in Fitzgerald's novel, Daisy Fay, whose beguil-
ing sexuality proves to be sterile illusion; and this instance
of common naming is given increased importance by its
appearance again in *The Day of the Locust*, in which Faye
Greener is a vacant Venus.

Myrtle Wilson, like Fay Doyle, is married to a pathetic failure of a man. Wilson pumps gas, and Pete Doyle
reads gas meters, but neither is fueled with any vitality or
has any sense of direction in his life. Wilson, according to
Myrtle, "doesn't even know he's alive," and Doyle, as his
wife says, "is all dried up." Their sexually starved wives
cheat on them, and then, in the grotesque endings the
husband-failure insanely shoots the hero. The absurdist
climax of *The Great Gatsby* becomes the ultimate absurdist joke of *Miss Lonelyhearts*. A death theme is pervasive
in *The Great Gatsby*, as it is again in *Miss Lonelyhearts*,
not only because the heroes must die but also because the
cultures themselves are dead, and any attempt to transcend them is doomed to failure.

V. S. Pritchett has described *Miss Lonelyhearts* as an
"American fable," and it is as a fable, with an intricate
miniaturization of effect, that frequently calls *The Great
Gatsby* to mind. Quite apart from the similarity of at least
two of the principal characters and of the endings, the
novels group together as very artful works belonging to a
special, very limited tradition in modern American fiction. The fable dimension of the novels derives in part
from their quest themes and quester heroes whose failures
reveal the most elemental truths of their cultures. But it is
insinuated, too, in the dream forms of the works, the
"magical" realism they employ. The real worlds they
explore seem distorted, so that the meanness of life
becomes almost incredibly mean, menacing, evil–

although comic too. Meyer Wolfsheim, with his cuff buttons made of human molars, becomes a plausible figure in the bizarre world in which he appears. The sexually devouring Fay Doyle, whose arm is like a "thigh," can be credited in *Miss Lonelyhearts*, with its vision of radical dislocation. In each novel a limited number of characters drawn in caricature interact in a morally charged atmosphere. Good and evil are constantly involved in the tensions of the works, in which values have become inverted. Both "fables" have a quality of lightness and grace, yet have been intensely and powerfully focused, and are modern moralities.

Miss Lonelyhearts can be compared to *The Great Gatsby* in still other ways.[10] Both are strongly visualized and imagistic, and are structured dramatically, developing in a series of distinct scenes, with many chapters dominated by a single episode. Both are elegantly satirical, and show special finesse in their reproduction of vulgar people and their banal speech. Scenes in *The Great Gatsby* are comic and horrible at once, as in the scene at the Washington Heights apartment; and this dual quality informs *Miss Lonelyhearts*—in the letters written to Miss Lonelyhearts, for example, and in Miss Lonelyhearts's seduction by Fay Doyle. The sterility of women in *The Great Gatsby* is striking, and it is again in *Miss Lonelyhearts*, in which, as in Fitzgerald, sexuality is linked with death. In all of these respects Fitzgerald is a presence in the background of *Miss Lonelyhearts*, which, remarkably original as it is, yet does have a context in the American literature that immediately precedes it.

West's modernist vision of alienation in *Miss Lonelyhearts* is focused by its hero, "Miss L," and by New York, which has been captured with a foreshortened intensity. The job at which Miss Lonelyhearts works gives him what little personal identity he has but, ironically, it is essentially merely a purveying of illusion. His advice-giving is offered to the unhappy in lieu of real religious sureties, which have long since disappeared. The earlier Protestant faith that once bolstered the nation has by the opening of the novel become an anachronism. In its place spurious religious cults flourish in the West, like the "Liberal Church of America," which intimates the breakdown of religious authority. The burden of finding spiritual guidance has fallen upon the isolated individual, and the individual alone is helpless in a chaotic world.

Miss Lonelyhearts himself has been provided with a religious background, is the son of a Baptist minister, and has "an Old Testament look." His high, narrow forehead and long, fleshless nose give him the aspect of "the New England puritan." A curious feature of Miss Lonelyhearts, however, is that his Baptist father seems unreal. So, for that matter, does the younger sister he remembers briefly in one episode. He seems so remote from a real family that one has an impression that he never had any. As for New England, he appears unacquainted with it, is so urban in his conception that when he sets foot in the Connecticut countryside, it seems a wholly new world to him. Ordinarily a character having a religious background that seems merely putative would not be credible. Yet Miss Lonelyhearts can somehow be accepted, for it is as if his urbanization has wiped out his background, made it intangible, and obliterated it. He is now essentially without connections, either to the past or to the present—a modern "stranger," like Camus's Meursault.

Miss Lonelyhearts's removal from family and tradition is shared by the other characters in the novel. His girl friend Betty is depicted as a kind of "average" girl, but what is peculiar about her is that she gives no sense of having a family; she lives alone in the city, and seems to know no one other than Miss Lonelyhearts. Two "families" are shown in the work, the Shrikes and the Doyles, but they are nightmare versions of wedded life. Between husband and wife there is no communication. There is, indeed, a horrifying hostility in their relations. Fay Doyle feels no affection for her husband, is contemptuous of him as "a shrimp of a cripple," and betrays him sexually. Shrike and his wife despise each other, and live together in a state of sexual warfare. These marital partners are as much cut off from others as those who live by themselves, like the "clean old man." They are all devastatingly alone.

The letters Miss Lonelyhearts receives all center upon the isolation and helplessness of those who write them. Sick-of-it-all has been made pregnant yet again by her husband, a "religious" Catholic who will not permit her to have an abortion, although she has been advised by her doctor that she will die in giving birth again, and her kidneys ache agonizingly. A letter from Harold S., fifteen, informs Miss Lonelyhearts that his sister, thirteen, a deaf mute, has been sexually abused on the roof of their building by a stranger, but is "afraid to tell mother on account of her being liable to beat Gracie up." On a previous occasion, when little Gracie tore her dress, her parents had locked her in a closet for two days. Furthermore, if the boys on the block hear that she has been molested "they will say dirty things like they did on Pee Wee Conors sister the time she got caught in the lots." These letters suggest an almost insane lack of caring or of compassion toward those who have every right to look for understanding.

The most horrendous of the letters is from Broad Shoulders, married to a man who, at different times, has deserted her and refused to support her and their children. While living with her he hides under the bed all day, lying in his own "dirt," waiting to frighten her to death when, cleaning under the bed, she comes upon him. She is so "frighted" by him that she becomes temporarily paralyzed from the waist down. At the end of the letter she reveals that a male boarder she has taken in so that she will be able to meet the rent "tries to make me bad and as there is nobody in the house when he comes home drunk on Saturday night I don't know what to do." In the letters of Broad Shoulders and the others, one finds only a failure of communication between people—between husbands and wives, children and parents, children and their peers.

Miss Lonelyhearts is in the same situation as those who apply to him for help. He is alone, feels his own helplessness, and is gripped by fear. When the novel opens, this fear has already taken hold of him; he is obsessional, and committed to what he himself calls a "Christ complex." *Miss Lonelyhearts* is, in part, a study of a neurotic personality. Even within his own mind, Miss Lonelyhearts doubts himself, the role he is steadily impelled to assume. In the complicated character doubling of the novel, Shrike, the mocker, is a projection of a part of himself. Shrike is a "satyr," while Miss Lonelyhearts has a chin like a "cloven hoof"; and no more than Shrike can he will away his animal nature, his frustration, the inner violence he feels.

West's linking of Miss Lonelyhearts and Shrike occurs early in the novel in the course of two parallel scenes that follow one another. In the first, Miss Lonelyhearts goes to Delehanty's speakeasy, where he meets Shrike. Before long Miss Farkis, Shrike's latest girl friend, appears and Shrike, who has already described her chief attributes for Miss Lonelyhearts by drawing a pair of breasts in the air, reduces her further upon introduction, "making her bow as a ventriloquist does his doll." They begin to talk, but when Miss Farkis attempts to join in the discussion, Shrike raises his fist "as though to strike her." He delivers a blasphemous "sermon" while caressing her body, at the conclusion of which, in an extraordi-

nary image, he buries "his triangular face like the blade of
a hatchet in her neck." He first reduces her to a sexual
object, and then vents his anger and violence upon her. In
a scene that appears soon after this one, Miss
Lonelyhearts goes to visit Betty, hoping that she may
help to restore his troubled spirit. But once with her, he
seems to taunt her for her sexuality, and with sadistic
cruelty reaches under her robe and gives a sharp tug to her
breast. He delivers a kind of "sermon" on his Christ complex as he touches her shoulder "threateningly," and she
raises her arm "as though to ward off a blow." In these
scenes Miss Lonelyhearts and Shrike appear as figures in
parallel, in threatening relationship to the women to
whom they turn for solace.

Throughout the novel Miss Lonelyhearts and Shrike
are played off against one another as would-be "believer"
and as "denier." Miss Lonelyhearts, as a spiritual coun-
selor to suffering humanity, has already begun to put
himself in the place of Christ, and Shrike has adopted the
role of Antichrist. The two are brought into tense,
dramatic conjunction in the opening paragraph, as Miss
Lonelyhearts stares at a piece of white cardboard on
which Shrike has had printed an ironic prayer to "Miss
L":

> Soul of Miss L, glorify me.
> Body of Miss L, nourish me.
> Blood of Miss L, intoxicate me.
> Tears of Miss L, wash me.
> Oh good Miss L, excuse my plea,
> And hide me in your heart,
> And defend me from mine enemies,
> Help me, Miss L, help me, help me.
> In saecula saeculorum. Amen.

Shrike's prayer is a parody of the "Anima Christi," or
"Soul of Christ," from Ignatius Loyola's *Spiritual Exer-*

cise; and it identifies Miss Lonelyhearts as a saint, after the pattern of Loyola. Loyola, who founded the Society of Jesus (the Jesuit order), zealously served the cause of Christ, and through discipline and desire for sacrifice made himself a master of the spiritual life. Miss Lonelyhearts, too, is a defender of Christ, and desires to serve the spiritually needy.

After reading the prayer card, and the letters to him from a number of desperate people in the city, Miss Lonelyhearts goes out to Delehanty's, stopping on the way to meditate in the little park. The condition of life seems to him like that of a "desert" as he enters the park at the "North Gate"[11]–an allusion to Ezra Pound's "Lament of the Frontier Guard," a vision of isolation in a ruined world that begins "By the North Gate, the wind blows full of sand." This saint in a modern urban desert is beset by doubt, yet clings to the idea of attaining spiritual enlightenment. As he enters the park, however, "the shadow of a lamppost that lay on the path . . . pierced him like a spear," which implies that this enlightenment may only be a lonely martyrdom. In Delehanty's he is again confronted by Shrike, and another saint is mentioned, St. Thomas Aquinas, who sought to bridge the gap between spirit and body. Almost immediately, in another of his deflating parodies, Shrike declares that he is himself a saint ("I walk on my own water"), and he delivers a sermon discrediting religion, while he fondles Miss Farkis.

This early antithetical linking of Miss Lonelyhearts and Shrike continues on thereafter through the rest of the novel. Miss Lonelyhearts leaves Delehanty's for his bare room that is like a monk's cell. It has no furnishings, except for an effigy of Christ at the foot of his bed, and is "as full of shadows as an old steel engraving," or religious etching. It is in this room that Miss Lonelyhearts has hallucinatory dreams and fever, and chants "Christ, Christ,

Jesus Christ" while looking at the "image that hung on the wall." Shrike enters Miss Lonelyhearts's room twice in the course of the novel, each time with disturbing effect. On the first occasion, Miss Lonelyhearts has suffered a breakdown and is nursed by Betty, who attempts to restore him with her own version of order. At this point Shrike bursts in drunkenly and, after Betty leaves, delivers a harangue, citing the possible avenues of escape available to him, while denying the efficacy of each in turn. The Church, he declares, is the only hope, and he dictates an imaginary, cynical letter to Christ, calling for help for Miss Lonelyhearts. He thus pushes Miss Lonelyhearts ever closer to despair.

Shrike appears in the room a second time late in the novel, again drunk, with a group of others. He rushes Miss Lonelyhearts off to his apartment to take part in a game that he has devised called "Everyman his own Miss Lonelyhearts," in which he will produce letters from the newspaper file, written by the most wretched, and ask Miss Lonelyhearts to provide "an absolute value and *raison d'être*." It is worth noting that when Shrike bursts into the room, Miss Lonelyhearts is caught naked, since in the scene that follows he is, in effect, stripped naked by Shrike, challenged in public in an entertainment which implies that his column of solace to the bereft is itself only a parlor game. What is more, he asks the delayed question of how it is possible to love humanity. One of the letters is from an elderly woman who has just lost her sole source of support, wears heavy boots on her torn, bleeding feet, and has rheum in her eyes. "Have you room in your heart for her?" Shrike asks devastatingly. He accidentally reveals a letter, furthermore, that has just come from Pete Doyle, threatening to blow Miss Lonelyhearts's brains out. Doyle is the very image of suffering humanity that Miss Lonelyhearts has attempted to succor, but cannot be loved because he is an incoherent monstrosity.

The scene ends with "the gospel according to Shrike," his Antichrist version of what life really consists of. In the "gospel," Shrike envisions Miss Lonelyhearts's passage through life as a sordid ordeal, a struggle to realize a high ideal that is based on illusion. In the final pages of the novel, in fever, Miss Lonelyhearts believes that a miracle has occurred and that, Christlike, he can minister to the abject with his love. With outstretched arms, he approaches Pete Doyle, then making his way awkwardly up the stairway, and is shot to death by him. In this final scene Miss Lonelyhearts's outstretched arms have the iconography of Christ on the cross.

R. W. B. Lewis, in *Trials of the Word*, has commented on Shrike as the novel's Antichrist, and his observations warrant quoting at length:

The novella moves unfalteringly between nightmare and actuality, its tone between horror and jesting; which is West's exemplary way of apprehending *our* world as under the dominion of a contemporary Antichrist. . . . It is Shrike who rules over and preys upon an urban scene composed of the heartless, the violent, and the wretched. And it is Shrike who pits himself against the would-be imitator of Christ, the hopeless columnist we know only by his pen name Miss Lonelyhearts, and whom Shrike torments in particular by spoken parodies of the Eucharist—that holy *communion* after which Miss Lonelyhearts so yearns. . . . In a ludicrously ill-timed and feverish effort to embrace and hence to redeem by love at least one individual human victim—a crippled homosexual named Peter Doyle—Miss Lonelyhearts is accidentally shot and killed; and in the abrasively ironic eschatology of this novella, the field is left to the further machinations of the Antichrist. But Shrike, consummate satirist though he is, is at the same time an object of satire—and the field of his triumph is no more than a frozen chaos.[12]

Lewis presents his case for Shrike as the Antichrist of the novel extremely well, but he does not quite grasp Shrike's role. Shrike does bear a likeness to the Antichrist, but it is part of West's larger intention that he is not the Antichrist himself, any more than Miss Lonelyhearts is the Nazarene. An Antichrist, or devil, does claim the world of *Miss Lonelyhearts* as his dominion, but Shrike is as much his victim as "Miss L." Shrike suffers from the same exacerbated rawness of nerves as Miss Lonelyhearts, and the very shrillness of his refusal of belief (his name could almost read "shriek") indicates that he is gripped by a similar hysteria. Nor does he triumph, however emptily, in the novel. Shrike preaches a cynical gospel of pure sensation; but what is striking about him is that his reduction of life to the sexual, or purely physical, brings him no pleasure. He is gnawed by torment in each of his appearances in the novel, and in one revealing moment, when he speaks of his life with his wife, his masklike "dead pan" breaks, and "pain actually crept into his voice." Rather than being the Antichrist of the novel, as Lewis mistakenly assumes, he is Miss Lonelyhearts's fellow sufferer.

Although he never appears, an Antichrist does rule in the work. He is the lord of disorder, and he possesses terrifying, even absolute, power. This "devil" is implied in Miss Lonelyhearts's reveries of his childhood, in which "something had stirred within him" when he shouted Christ's name, and he is tempted to bring it to life. But what this "something" is that stirs in him is made to seem fearful, as if the revelation he awaits may be wholly unlike that which he dimly imagines. Shifting forward to the present in his reverie, Miss Lonelyhearts reflects that "he knew now what this thing was—hysteria, a snake whose scales are tiny mirrors in which the dead world takes on a semblance of life. And how dead the world is. . . . He wondered if hysteria were really too steep a price to pay for bringing it to life." West's imagery evokes a world of the living dead, beyond reclaiming, and in the possession of a demon-snake whose mirror-scales flash illusion. In his room, when Miss Lonelyhearts begins to chant Christ's name, "the snake started to uncoil in his brain, he became frightened and closed his eyes." In the final chapter, a shout of "Christ, Christ" echoes through his brain, as his room is transformed into a vision of grace and he talks to God, telling him that he now "accepts" life. A moment later he walks out of the room to confront chaos and violence. Just before this scene Shrike had announced to the group at his apartment: "This is only one more attempt against him by the devil. He has spent his life struggling with the arch fiend for our sakes, and he shall triumph. I mean Miss Lonelyhearts, not the devil." But it is the devil, of course, who presides at Miss Lonelyhearts's undoing, who punishes his presumption, his attempt to quicken the dead world into life.

Miss Lonelyhearts's Christ delusion is implied throughout the work, and it is often dramatized on the level of sexual fear. In an early chapter, Miss Lonelyhearts, as a college student, discusses the existence of God with two other young men in a dormitory room, after which, on a drinking spree, they go out at dawn to sacrifice a lamb in a religious ritual. The sacrifice of the lamb takes places in the spring, and is a rite of purification. But they cannot believe as much in the innocence of the lamb as they would like, and drink heavily to work up a delusionary excitement. Not surprisingly, the sacrifice of the lamb is botched, becoming a brutal killing, an early undermining of Miss Lonelyhearts's yearning for transcendence. But what should be noted about the scene, too, is its sexual undercurrent. On the way to the ritual, the young men sing an obscene version of "Mary Had a Little Lamb," which presumably substitutes for "lamb," a four-letter epithet for the female sexual organ. In the nursery rhyme, Mary and her "innocent" lamb are identified (one always accompanies the other), and there is some suggestion that it is the female herself whom Miss Lonelyhearts seeks to restore to innocence, to purge of sexuality—an effort that is doomed to failure and drives him into a violent state of rage.

Miss Lonelyhearts's yearning for innocence and the violence associated with it are also seen in the later chapter entitled "Miss Lonelyhearts and the Clean Old Man." The chapter begins at Delehanty's, where male patrons take obvious pleasure in relating how women writers, claiming to have aesthetic ideals, are sexually assaulted and brutally demeaned. This brutalization is a form of revenge by men for the painful loss of their own earlier ideals—a demand that those claiming to ideals be made to confront the sordid emptiness and horror at the basis of life. At one point in the scene Miss Lonelyhearts himself has a reverie of his young sister as she dances to the music of Mozart, a brief vision of innocence and grace that is shattered when he is struck in the face by another man—an act of senseless, anonymous urban anger.

After Miss Lonelyhearts leaves the speakeasy with his friend Gates, he directs his own anger at an old homosexual in a comfort station. First at the comfort station and then at an Italian speakeasy where they take him, they taunt him and demand to know the story of his unhappy life. The old man, who carries a cane and dresses as if he had some claims to respectability, is not forthcoming with a confession, and Miss Lonelyhearts becomes virtually hysterical, twisting the old man's arm until the man screams. Miss Lonelyhearts here continues a pattern begun early in the chapter. He attempts to strip the old man of his genteel pretensions and make him confess to the loneliness, degradation, and suffering of his life.

But why, when he is balked in this attempt, should Miss Lonelyhearts lose his self-control so totally? His response to the old man, it should be noted, is complicated by the pity he wishes to feel for him, a pity mingled

with evident disgust. He seeks to enter into his degradation, to establish a spiritual union with him. His spiritual
failure quickly turns into rage and physical assault. Surely
his rage is due to the "doubling" that is intimated to exist
between them. The homosexuality to which the old man
will not admit also seems present, at least latently, in Miss
Lonelyhearts, whose spiritual protestations are comparable, in a way, to the old man's genteel clothes. In this context, Miss Lonelyhearts's rage against the old man's
refusal to confess is an attack upon himself, upon his own
duplicity.

The old man in the comfort station will not allow Miss
Lonelyhearts to "love" him, but later he finds an ideal
candidate for his spiritual embrace, Pete Doyle. Doyle is
undisguisedly wretched, a cripple with a cane and a built-
up shoe, which he drags behind him, making "many
waste motions, like those of a partially destroyed insect."
He is unsuccessful with women, and called "a queer guy"
by his wife, who disdains and mistreats him. Although
repelled by Fay Doyle, even though he allows her to
seduce him, Miss Lonelyhearts is much attracted to her
husband, the very image of human infirmity. To "love"
Pete Doyle, the least and most lowly placed of humanity,
is, in the context of Father Zosima's sermon, to "see
God."

The courtship of Miss Lonelyhearts and Pete Doyle is
grotesquely comic, perhaps the most grotesque courtship
in American literature. In a late scene set at Delehanty's,
Miss Lonelyhearts meets Doyle for the first time, and
Doyle produces a letter he has written to him and now lets
him read. The letter, which begins "I am a cripple 41 years
of age which I have been all my life," recounts the various
indignities he has suffered, and asks "but what I want to
no is what is the whole stinking business for." Even if
inarticulately, Doyle asks the big questions: What is life
all about? Why, if there is a just God, do human beings

suffer meaninglessly? Miss Lonelyhearts experiences an identification with him as his double, a physical cripple as he is a spiritual one. Hence their first embrace. "When Miss Lonelyhearts was puzzling out the crabbed writing," West comments,

Doyle's damp hand accidentally touched his under the table. He jerked away, but then drove his hand back and forced it to clasp the cripple's. After finishing the letter, he did not let go, but pressed it firmly with all the love he could manage. At first the cripple covered his embarrassment by disguising the meaning of the clasp with a handshake, but soon he gave in to it and they sat silently, hand in hand.

The courtship is continued at the Doyle house, where the two go after leaving Delehanty's. Mrs. Doyle makes aggressive advances to Miss Lonelyhearts, who fends her off, and when she leaves the room for a moment he smiles "beatifically" at the cripple. Doyle extends his hand, and Miss Lonelyhearts clasps it, smiling. They are still holding hands when Mrs. Doyle reenters the room and comments: "What a sweet pair of fairies you guys are." At this point, Miss Lonelyhearts delivers a sermon to the effect that "Christ is love," which makes the Doyles feel embarrassed. He is already overwrought, at the evident failure of the Christlike part he has attempted to play, when Doyle is sent out to buy a bottle of whiskey, and in Doyle's absence he is set upon sexually by Mrs. Doyle, whom he beats in a blind rage and then flees from their house. His rage is triggered by his obvious failure to establish a spiritual union with Doyles. His "love" message is mocked by sexuality: Mrs. Doyle's rapacious heterosexuality and the latent homosexuality hinted at in his handholding with her husband. His attempt to intervene in the lives of the Doyles leads not to love but to his own frenzied beating of Mrs. Doyle, and to Doyle's crazed response (his belief that he had come to their house

to rape his wife, was not the redeemer he claimed to be)
that sends him to Miss Lonelyhearts's door with gun in
hand. At the top of the stairs, in his final delusion, Miss
Lonelyhearts reaches out to embrace the cripple, just as
Betty appears, and confusion follows. In a way he is killed
not even by Doyle but by the accidental discharge of the
gun, a meaningless, impersonal act suggesting the irrational nature of life that Miss Lonelyhearts has attempted to
order with "love."

Miss Lonelyhearts's "Christ complex" has inevitably
invited Freudian interpretations, beginning with Stanley
Edgar Hyman's influential discussion of the final scene:

> It is of course a homosexual tableau–the men locked in embrace
> while the woman stands helplessly by–and behind his other
> miseries Miss Lonelyhearts has a powerful latent homosexual-
> ity. . . . We could, if we so chose, write Miss Lonelyhearts' case
> history before the novel begins. Terrified of his stern religious
> father, identifying with his soft loving mother, the boy
> renounces his phallicism out of castration anxiety–a classic
> Oedipus complex. In these terms the Shrikes are Miss
> Lonelyhearts' Oedipal parents, abstracted as the father's loud
> voice and the mother's tantalizing breast. The scene at the end of
> Miss Lonelyhearts' date with Mary Shrike is horrifying and
> superb. Standing outside her apartment door, suddenly over-
> come with passion, he strips her naked under her fur coat while
> she keeps talking mindlessly of her mother's death, mumbling
> and repeating herself, so that Shrike will not hear the sudden
> silence and come out. Finally Mary agrees to let Miss
> Lonelyhearts in if Shrike is not home, goes inside, and soon
> Shrike peers out the door, wearing only the tops of his pajamas.
> It is the child's Oedipal vision perfectly realized.[13]

One would not even have to endorse Hyman's Oedipal
reading of the scene between Miss Lonelyhearts and the
Shrikes to be aware of how devastatingly it comments on
Miss Lonelyhearts's sexuality. As he hears footsteps
approaching the door, Miss Lonelyhearts "limps" behind

the projection of an elevator shaft. The shaft itself is phallic, Shrike's phallicism is startlingly evident in his sudden
appearance wearing only his pajama tops, and Miss
Lonelyhearts cowers in the shadows of the shaft like a
guilty child. Clearly this final moment of the chapter
reveals Miss Lonelyhearts as sexually maimed.

West's concerns in *Miss Lonelyhearts*, including prob-
lematic identity and violence, can be noticed in the pervasive imagery of the novel. In the opening prayer, which
introduces the theme of the work, a key word is "heart":
"hide me in your heart / And defend me from mine
enemies." The name Miss Lonelyhearts itself, even if
ironic, makes one continually conscious of the heart, the
seat of compassion and love. At one point in the work,
Miss Lonelyhearts "killed his great understanding heart
by laughing," and in a dream sequence, he attempts to
shape the paraphernalia in a pawnshop window into the
shape of a heart. But an imagery running counter to it
is that of stone or rock, implying an inability to feel—an
extension of what West, in *Balso Snell*, had called the
"Mundane Millstone." At the beginning Miss
Lonelyhearts, discouraged, remembers Shrike's comment that he should give his readers "stones." "Give us
this day our daily stone" becomes a parodic version of the
Lord's Prayer. All that Miss Lonelyhearts can feel as he
enters the little park is "the stone that had formed in his
gut."

The menacing buildings that surround the park are the
work of a civilization of "stone breakers," and it is
implied that nature has retaliated upon this culture of
"forced rock and tortured steel," in which the natural, the
ability to feel spontaneously and purely, has become distorted and is transmuted into hardness and inhumanity.
Fay Doyle's legs are like boulders, enormous grind-
stones, and late in the work Miss Lonelyhearts imagines

that he has come into possession of a faith that will protect him from the brutalization that is everywhere about him, a faith analogous to the rock of faith on which the Church was built. But the rock he possesses within himself merely deadens him to external reality, to the catastrophe awaiting him at the stairway landing.

Breasts appear with extraordinary frequency, but rather than suggesting natural innocence or tender maternity, they have a purely sexual connotation. Fay Doyle, a voluptuary, has breasts of mammoth size. Miss Farkis means no more to Shrike than a pair of breasts, and Mary Shrike uses her breasts as a form of sexual enticement (an enticement made grotesque by the fact that her mother had died of cancer of the breast). Miss Lonelyhearts sadistically twists Betty's nipple, as if to pluck it violently from her body, and elsewhere parts of the human anatomy are wrenched from the whole, or made to resemble other, disparate parts of the anatomy. Betty's upraised arms pull her breasts up "until they were like pink-tipped thumbs," and other allusions to breasts take strangely nonorganic forms, as in the oddly memorable reference to the naked girl in the mineral water poster whose nipples are "like tiny red hats."

Religious imagery and allusions abound in the novel, but they all suggest an inaccessible tradition, twisted into sterile modern forms. Beginning with the opening paragraph, in which Miss Lonelyhearts reads Shrike's prayer card addressed to a secular Christ, the newsroom of the New York *Post-Dispatch* is evoked as a modern temple of faith, to which the wretched send their letters that are like prayers for deliverance. That the newsroom, the New Church, cannot aid them is implied immediately in the image of the newspaper that is blown in the wind over the park "like a kite with a broken spine." The newspaper's broken spine introduces the crippling theme, and by the end the newspaper is associated with outbursts of violence. Fay Doyle uses a rolled-up newspaper as a club with which to beat her husband, and he, in turn, goes to Miss Lonelyhearts's room with a gun concealed under a newspaper.

A number of religiously connotative names appear in the novel, but those who bear them imply merely a religious ideal that has become incoherent. Mary and Joseph are present in the childless, frigid Mary Shrike, and in Joseph Zemp (alluded to in a newspaper clipping) who is slain in an argument over a trifling amount of money. Doyle has the same name as Peter, who founded the Christian church on the rock of faith. Miss Lonelyhearts's friend Gates has a name with religious associations, but he merely accompanies Miss Lonelyhearts to a comfort station where they torment the "clean old man," hoping to wring a sordid story from him as the real "truth" of his life. The life of the city, as it is imagined in *Miss Lonelyhearts*, is cramped and claustrophobic. There are no real homes in it, only apartments and rooms that seem hardly lived in, or that have hostile or horrifying associations. Delehanty's speakeasy is the single social center shown in the novel, and it is "illegitimate," entered through an "armored door" with a small aperture that, on the other side, reveals a glowingly red, bloodshot eye. In the color symbolism of *Miss Lonelyhearts*, nature has a gray, oppressive shading. "The gray sky" looks "as if it had been rubbed with a soiled eraser," obliterating any meaning that might be found in it. At the same time, the color red appears frequently, and has been associated with sex and violence.

In a variety of images West employs, innocence ends inevitably in disillusionment and animality. No vegetation grows in the little park, and if flowers were to spring up, watered by the "tears" of the city's inhabitants, they would smell of "feet." The imagery of the rose, that reminder of Christ's perfect love, appears early when Miss Lonelyhearts, thinking of what he will say to the despondent letter writers, reflects that "his heart was a rose and in his skull another rose bloomed." Yet later he twists Betty's breast as a rose that he will pluck, and wear in his buttonhole as if it were no more than an artificial decoration. In the final scene, Miss Lonelyhearts's room seems full of grace, "as clean as the innersides of the inner petals of a newly forced rosebud," but the vision proves delusionary and is quickly followed by his death.

Shrike remarks that somewhere in the jungle of entrails within man's body "lives a bird called the soul," yet Shrike's own name is taken from the "butcher bird," which impales its victims on thorns before tearing them apart with its hooked beak. Shrike bears the insignia of the trinity in his triangularly shaped head, but his face is, in fact, "a dead, gray triangle." In one of his many parodies, Shrike describes God as "Father, Son, and Silver Wire-haired Terrier"; and at times West plays with the idea of the dog as God spelled backwards, an anagram of man's condition. When Miss Lonelyhearts tells Betty hysterically that he is a "humanity lover," he is said to "bark" out the words; and later, in one of the novel's most harrowing scenes, Pete Doyle is beaten by his wife with a rolled-up newspaper, which he seizes in his teeth while rolling on the floor like a dog.

Sadistic violence and cruelty are everywhere present in West's tropes of weapons and sharp blades and knives. Miss Lonelyhearts is pierced by a shadow "spear." Shrike's face is like the blade of a hatchet. The husband of Broad Shoulders leaves hammers and knives under his pillow to "fright" her. In the pawnshop window, in Miss Lonelyhearts's dream, "a tortured high light twisted on the blade of a gift knife." He drives the effigy of Christ into the wall of his room with a "spike," hoping to see it writhe. Shrike tells Miss Lonelyhearts that sleeping with his wife "is like sleeping with a knife in one's groin," an obvious image of castration.

Those who write to Miss Lonelyhearts are women

who have been oppressed and mistreated by men, yet other women in the novel are men's victimizers. They seem sexually damaged in one respect or another, and use their sexuality in a way that prohibits any exchange of genuine feeling or intimacy. Miss Farkis has a name that suggests "far-kiss," or a remoteness from feeling. She appears only briefly and hardly speaks at all, but there is nevertheless a mannishness about her that is striking. She has "thick ankles, big hands, a powerful body, a man's haircut," and she acknowledges her introduction to Miss Lonelyhearts "with a masculine handshake." She is not necessarily implied to be a lesbian (although she could be), but she is clearly sexually ambivalent. Mary Shrike is even less at ease with her sexuality. Although she dresses in a way that coquettishly calls attention to her breasts, she is actually frigid, and does not know how to be natural. She wears a sexy garment, "a tight, shiny dress," yet it resembles "glass-covered steel." Lacking spontaneity and on the deepest level hating sex, Mary Shrike is as sterile as the world that made her and that she reflects. Fay Doyle is not repressed, like Mary Shrike, but rather deranged in her femininity, a sexual warrior who destroys her husband and fills Miss Lonelyhearts with fear.

In *The Bostonians*, Henry James dramatized a cultural breakdown in late nineteenth-century America through a derangement in the relation of the sexes, with masculinized women and effeminized men who cannot come together with any ease or naturalness. *Miss Lonelyhearts* carries this analogy between cultural breakdown and sexual dislocation even further, envisioning a world in which embitterment over the loss of faith and ideals produces a warlike relationship of the sexes, the maiming of both men and women alike.

West's characters are all stunted half persons or nonpersons who grope for an identity or sense of wholeness that they cannot find. The protagonist has no name except the pen name he uses in his column, one with a gender that would seem to cancel out his manhood. Implying her incompleteness, Betty has no last name; and Shrike has no first name, only a last one that limits his identity by likening him to a nonhuman creature, a ferociously assaultive bird. The people who write to Miss Lonelyhearts have no real names, only generic labels, like Sick-of-it-all. Miss Farkis has no first name, and is reduced to nonentity by Shrike's use of her as a ventriloquist's doll. Mary Shrike, Fay, and Pete Doyle have names, but they do not know who or what they are. The features of Pete's face are incoherent. His eyes fail to balance, and his mouth is not under his nose; his forehead is shaped like a chin and his chin is like a diminutive forehead. When he talks his speech makes no sense. "He was giving birth," West remarks, "to groups of words that lived inside of him as things, a jumble of retorts he had meant to make when insulted and the private curses against fate that experience had taught him to swallow."

These characters have more in common with the characters in *Balso Snell* than one might think since, like the characters in the earlier novel, they are unable to become "real," to enter intelligibly into life. Mary Shrike is a good example of this. Miss Lonelyhearts joins her in an excursion to a nightclub called the El Gaucho, where an orchestra plays a Cuban rhumba, and waiters are dressed as South American cowboys. The nightclub is like a theater, which offers romantic illusion as reality. Its guitars, bright shawls, exotic foods, and outlandish costumes are, as West remarks, "part of the business of dreams," a form of escape for people from the emptiness of their lives. In this atmosphere, Mary offers herself to Miss Lonelyhearts "in a series of formal, impersonal gestures," a "pantomime" of real emotion. Miss Lonelyhearts has been intrigued by a medal she wears on a chain around her neck, and at the El Gaucho, in a fine touch, is at last.able to glimpse the medal, which turns out to be a high-school athletic award for first place in the one-hundred-yard dash. It is preposterous that this medal lying in the cleavage between her breasts should be an athletic award. Presumably it would be something of a religious or at least personal nature that would involve tenderness or sentiment.

Mary Shrike's romantic daydream at the El Gaucho is followed by a horrifying scene in front of her apartment door, where she is literally stripped naked by Miss Lonelyhearts. Not wanting to let her husband know, through a long awkward silence that she is being seduced by Miss Lonelyhearts, she mumbles in a kind of chant: "My mother died of cancer of the breast. . . . She died leaning over a table. My father was a portrait painter. He led a gay life. He mistreated my mother. She had cancer of the breast. . . . " Her recall of her "interesting" parents is a romanticization of a life that is wholly without meaning. The reality of her situation is that she has just been stripped by one man, and will soon be "raped" by another, waiting at the other side of the door.

If Mary Shrike has no real existence at all, Betty has hardly more. Her neatness or orderliness precludes any consciousness of suffering or of the irrational in life. She wishes to "adjust" Miss Lonelyhearts to her own painfully limited vision. When he experiences a spiritual collapse, she appears at his room and spoon-feeds him chicken soup as if he had a cold. Her stunting is implied when Miss Lonelyhearts turns on her viciously, denouncing her "wide-eyed little mother act." It *is* an act, insofar as it is a confining role she plays that keeps her from having to confront the madness of life.

When Miss Lonelyhearts accompanies her for a weekend in the country, Betty is depicted as an unfallen Eve, set against an Edenic landscape. It is, however, an Eden in decay. The hamlet not far from the retreat is named Monkstown, but it has already been corrupted by the secular. Miss Lonelyhearts goes there to pick up newspapers, a reminder of the encroachment of devitalized dreams. He stops at the Aw-Kum-On Garage, which suggests a leering overture to quick sex; and the comments of the garage man about "Yids" implies an ugly division among men, a loss of the ideal of brotherhood. The retreat itself is shadowed menacingly by "deep shade" and silence that is like "a funereal hush." The new green leaves on the trees shine in the sun "like an army of little metal shields," and the sound of a thrush singing is "like that of a flute choked with saliva." Nature seems contaminated, its innocence at the verge of being lost. The chapter ends with Miss Lonelyhearts's sexual act with Betty, which brings about the "fall" of this Adam and Eve. Once their relationship becomes overtly sexual, there is no longer an Eden to which they can return.

Before long, Betty realizes that she is pregnant, and she adopts another role, like that of Janey Davenport in *Balso Snell*, playing the part of the girl in trouble, derived in type from romance magazines. She breaks the news to Miss Lonelyhearts at a soda fountain where they go on a date, drinking strawberry sodas through straws—a parody of "adolescent love." Her "light blue" dress, at the same time, intimates that she is a version of the Virgin Mary, removed from sexuality "immaculately." As Virgin Mary and "adolescent girl," Betty will marry Miss Lonelyhearts, and they will have a happy future in Connecticut, like a couple in a romance magazine story. In this projective escape, Betty is reduced to the dimensionless status of her decorative "party dress." Miss Lonelyhearts, West remarks sardonically, "begged the party dress to marry him, saying all the things it expected to hear, all the things that went with strawberry sodas and farms in Connecticut."

But the most dimensionless of the female characters is

Fay Doyle, who derives from Mary McGeeney, at the end of *Balso Snell*, when she surrenders to the urgings of sex, muttering "yes, yes" to its biological dictates. A motif that prepares for her appearance is that of nature as it continually tends toward decay and formlessness, the "entropy" West refers to that is a more powerful and relentless process than man's ability to create order. Comically, when she seduces Miss Lonelyhearts, she is captured as an embodiment of the mindless, instinctual drives of entropic nature. Her call to him to hurry is a "sea moan," and when she lies beside him she heaves, "tidal, moon-driven." When Miss Lonelyhearts leaves the bed after their sexual experience, he is "like an exhausted swimmer, leaving the surf."

What is striking about her sexuality is that it is without intelligence or form, and is a gruesome distortion of the "feminine." When she first appears in the little park, she is dressed in a strangely mismatching outfit that includes a plaid skirt and Tam O'Shanter, as if she were a member of a Scottish marching regiment, and she is said to resemble "a police captain." Although Miss Lonelyhearts engages in sex with her, it is she who makes the aggressive advances and who overpowers *him*. Her mindlessness is revealed in her account to Miss Lonelyhearts of her life with her husband. She tells of having been given a child out of wedlock by a certain Tony Benelli, a "dirty dago" she thought was a "gent." Doyle marries her, providing her with a husband and her daughter Lucy with a father; yet rather than feeling gratitude, she demeans her husband through a need to assert herself.

She even takes little Lucy to Benelli's home, where she stages a scene, shouting "he's the father of my child" in front of Benelli and his wife, before the Benellis threaten to call the police and she "beats it." Later, at home, she tells the child that she should remember that "her real papa" was a man named Tony Benelli and that he had wronged her, a story inspired by "too many movies." Her playing the aggrieved woman such as she has seen in films merely blinds her to her injury of her child and husband, whose fondness for the child she resents. She destroys his last sustaining illusion, that he is a father and adequate man; and in the "theatrical" scene that ensues the Doyles strike each other. When Doyle attempts to hit his wife with his cane he misses, falls onto the floor, and begins to cry pathetically. "The kid was on the floor crying too," she says, "and that set me off because the next thing I knew I was on the floor bawling too." In this scene of utter squalor and confusion, her sentimentality is again a means of dramatizing herself, so that she does not have to examine her own vacancy.

Perhaps the single most important line in *Miss Lonelyhearts* is spoken by one of the anonymous voices at Delehanty's. Miss Lonelyhearts is being discussed, and various opinions of his Christ fixation are put forward. One voice, however, stands out from the others in the insight it affords. "The trouble with him," the voice says, "the trouble with all of us, is that we have no outer life, only an inner one, and that by necessity." In the barrenness of their world, West's isolated characters are driven inward upon themselves, forced to embrace illusion; and living through illusion as they do they cannot establish contact with others. They are all participants in a Theater of the Absurd, acting out illusionary parts.

The principal theatrical roles have been assumed by Miss Lonelyhearts and Shrike, the two most sentient characters. They might be said to stand, respectively, for heart and head: Miss Lonelyhearts would come to terms with life through sympathy and compassion, Shrike attempts to deal with it through his hardened intelligence. One is a humanity lover, the other a God-hater. In each case, in the extremity of their attitudes, they become iso-

lated characters confined within, stunted by, the theatrical roles they assume. Even early in the work Miss
Lonelyhearts is identified as an actor. Shadows "curtain"
the arch that leads into the little park where he goes to
meditate on modern sainthood. In the ritual of the lamb's
sacrifice he plays the part ostentatiously of the priest, and
in his column he is an ersatz Christ. In each case, he pre-
tends to an identity he cannot justify in his actual experience. Referring to his column, Miss Lonelyhearts refers
to "the Christ business," and as such it is merely another
of the many commercialized dreams of escape from an
irreducible emptiness.

What one notices about Miss Lonelyhearts is that he
constantly drives himself to feel more than he can. In the
early scene in which he removes the effigy of Christ from
its backing and drives it into the wall with a spike, he
hopes to see it writhe, and is disturbed that Christ's
expression remains "decoratively placid." He himself
would wish to feel with great intensity, but can never feel
enough, so that he is conscious of his own spuriousness.
When he attempts to explain himself to Betty as a "humanity lover," he begins to shout at her, "accompanying
his shouts with gestures that were too appropriate, like
those of an old-fashioned actor." By the end of the scene,
in fact, he turns on her angrily and cries: "What's the matter, sweetheart? . . . Didn't you like the performance?"
When he attempts to enunciate his gospel of love to the
Doyles at their home, he forces his voice to shrillness,
until it becomes a "stage scream." This theatrical imagery
continually reminds the reader that Miss Lonelyhearts is
attempting a heroic role that eludes him.

Shrike, too, is highly theatrical. As a Christ-mocker,
he strikes attitudes, and is characteristically captured in
theatrical tableaux. He twice raises his fist to Miss Farkis,
a gesture that seems "frozen" like a camera still, and
buries his hatchetlike head in her neck in a "frozen"

moment that ends the chapter. A passage in the original version of this chapter, but removed in revision, reads: "Shrike and his stage, the speakeasy, made [Miss Lonelyhearts] feel that he was wandering, lost without hope of escape, among the scenery and costumes in the cellar of an ancient theatre."[14] Shrike is locked into his role just as Miss Lonelyhearts is locked into his. His illusion is that he can compensate for the loss of God and of spiritual values through a defiant hedonism. But hedonism is merely another escape dream, as he himself, at one point, notes; and for Shrike it is singularly and bitterly pleasureless. Shrike's shrillness is an attempt to kill the nerve of feeling, which mocks his attempt to find self-mastery through hardened intelligence alone. Inwardly divided, caught between a spirituality that is dead and a sexuality that is malignant, Miss Lonelyhearts and Shrike are "performers" unable to achieve an authentic sense of self.

West's conception of his characters as grotesque performers is at times accompanied by a vaudeville motif. Miss Lonelyhearts dreams that he is a magician juggling doorknobs on the stage of a crowded theater. At his command, they bleed, flower, and speak—a clownish parody of his role as a modern-day Christ. He attempts to create shapes out of pawnshop paraphernalia, performing in its window that is like a stage for onlookers. Although he makes spiritual claims, he is at various times the butt of low-comedy humor, particularly when he attempts to assert his manhood, a measure of his ability to control the world around him. His sex scene with Fay Doyle might have been put on the stage, its broad humor of gigantic woman versus small, inadequate man would draw the laughter of the crowd.

Shrike, too, has vaudeville associations. "He practiced a trick," West writes, "used much by moving-picture comedians—the dead pan"; regardless of his gestures, his face is always blank. He is an absurd clown with an inanimate face and a dead soul, a satirist whose ungodly jests are turned ultimately upon himself. Finally, Pete Doyle is a comic performer, however unwillingly. When he returns home, for instance, he is grabbed comically by his wife, who "shakes the breath out of him." In the end, he can only burlesque himself. When he brings Miss Lonelyhearts home, Mrs. Doyle makes sexual advances to his friend, and Pete "groans," exclaiming: "Ain't I the pimp, to bring a guy home for my wife?" He drops to his knees and does an imitation of a dog; and when Miss Lonelyhearts bends over to help him, Doyle tears open Miss Lonelyhearts's fly, rolling "over on his back, laughing wildly." His burlesque of himself as a pitiful cuckold is only too accurate a rendering of the disparity between the characters' yearning for a sense of meaning and the actual meaninglessness of their lives.

One would wonder what, in West's own experience and psychic makeup, could have produced such a bleak vision of life. One might speculate that its origins lay in West's own sense of exclusion from life and of sexual inadequacy. West's treatment of women is particularly revealing since, whether frigid or sexually devouring, they all seem threatening. Homosexuality also enters importantly into the work, and one would surmise that Miss Lonelyhearts's problem of latent homosexuality was also West's. Miss Lonelyhearts's passive-hysteric nature, certainly, carries the suggestion of some innermost hysteric tendency in the man who created him so powerfully. The very power of *Miss Lonelyhearts* attests to its having been written from tremulous nerves and acute inner anxieties. *Miss Lonelyhearts* has the quality of a waking dream, a truly and magnificently haunting one that is, in some ways, a sexual dream.

V. S. Pritchett has called *Miss Lonelyhearts* "very nearly faultless,"[15] but one could quibble with a few things. Betty finds that she is pregnant rather too quickly after she has sex with Miss Lonelyhearts, and the business of Pete Doyle's threatening letter, accidentally picked up with other mail and read by Shrike at the party, is perhaps too "managed." Doyle's appearance at Miss Lonelyhearts's building at the end, with gun in hand, is just possible, given his derangement and sense of betrayal, but because he is so passive, so hopelessly crushed, one wonders if he would be capable of this final outburst. More generally, the final three chapters have a sped-up hysteria that is slightly out of key with the earlier chapters of the novel. But these quibbles mean little compared to the deep impression of life the novel conveys. An astonishing performance, *Miss Lonelyhearts* is a work that an author, if he is exceptionally gifted and unusually fortunate, might write once in a lifetime.

Miss Lonelyhearts is a luminous and deeply compelling work that has great character conceptions, from "Miss L" himself to Shrike and the Doyles. The preposterous Fay Doyle is so inspired a conception that no other female character of a similar banality can compare with her in the whole range of twentieth-century American writing. Not since *The Great Gatsby* has a novel created its age with such merciless satire. Its craftsmanship and vivid style belong to the twenties, but its mood is distinctively part of the thirties. It is the most "original" novel to come out of the Depression, a "religious" work of macabre humor that searches into the dark places of modern loneliness. Its quality, finally, is its ambiguousness, its odd mixture of comedy and horror; its mingling of realism and fantasy; its exposure of Miss Lonelyhearts's illusion, yet its compassion for the "lost" and certitude of good cause for the sorrowing heart of Miss Lonelyhearts.

4

A Cool Million:
The Vaudeville of Apocalypse

During the early 1930s West wrote at least seven stories that were never finished or published, but have been preserved in manuscript and reveal his preoccupations of that time.[1] One of the most telling of these is "The Adventurer," which may draw on West's own youthful experiences in New York. Its first-person narrator, Joe Rucker, relates how he and some friends, as small boys, began to consort together in Central Park at night. "We used the trails then," he comments, "to spy on the grown people who hid in the brush. We would sit by the hour watching two men kiss or a woman masturbate. We would wait until they were at the height of their excitement, then suddenly shout foul names and run, yelling wildly." An interesting touch is that in these voyeuristic games Rucker turns the "wholesome" Scout Manual to subversive ends. "We were playing a game," he says, "that involved certain virtues (also found in the Scout Manual) such as knowing the signs and habits of our quarry, stalking, trailing, observing carefully, remaining absolutely still and so forth. . . . The climax of our hunt was savagely cruel and yet it was the only climax we could manage." This hunt, which ends in no real climax either in a sexual or any other sense, is implied to be a search for "reality." Originating in voyeurism, it is at several removes from life, and is refracted through a series of distancing lenses. The pubescent boys are not yet capable of adult experience, but even the adults they spy upon are themselves outcasts and fantasists.

Later, in his teens, as an order clerk in a wholesale grocery store, Joe has further "adventures," which consist of daydreams and memories of earlier daydreams that are replayed and elaborated upon in his imagination. His father, a janitor, sorts through rubbish sent down in dumbwaiters for momentoes of pleasure—dance cards, theater programs, gourmet menus—which he stores in barrels; and Joe, too, collects pleasurable fantasies, old "debris" that he hoards and sifts through over and over. At seventeen, as a messenger, he likes to pretend that his uniform is a disguise worn to fool his enemies. Between deliveries, he haunts the public library where he assumes imaginative disguises or identities. Eventually he comes to recognize "the corruption, the monstrosity" of the library, filled with others who burrow through dream images thrown up by the past. These people, with "rubbed, soiled faces," pursue "ten thousand deliriums." His father's barrel of ersatz memories, the fragmented dreams of those who lose themselves in books at the library, and his own fantasy life are, West declares, "The Apocalypse of the Second Hand!" At the end he returns to the park where he had "hunted" as a boy, to find it a congregating place of adults who seek out hiding places in the dense thickets. Appalled, he yet joins them, finds a secluded place to "lurk in the bush, hiding and dreaming." He is able to imagine but not to be, and his adult experience circles back to his childhood hunt for reality that has no resolution.

In "The Adventurer," West reveals a good deal about himself, but the story is revealing, too, in the use West makes of collective dreaming, projected through the experience of a youthful hero. In this sense, "The Adventurer" anticipates *A Cool Million*, in which the stunting of a young man, in his quest for life and reality, is related closely to the dream life of the masses. The dichotomy in "The Adventurer" between the outer and inner life is explored rather differently, but also revealingly, in two other stories of the same period, "Mr. Potts of Pottstown" and "The Sun, the Lady, and the Gas Station." In "Mr. Potts of Pottstown," the hero has a very strong dream life, even going so far as to form a local Hunt Club that feeds wholly on fantasy, since no game exists in the nearby woods. Before long a local lawyer forms an Alpine Club, also a creation of fantasy, in competition with Potts's club, and the members of the Hunt Club defect to the Alpine Club. Potts now girds himself to outdo his competitors by actually confronting reality. He outfits himself with apparel and gear for mountain climbing, and departs for the Swiss Alps. But what Potts discovers abroad is that the Alpine climbing is itself a dream.

As he is preparing to climb the Jungfrau, Potts hears a yodel that sounds strangely familiar:

"It's me, Jimmy Larkin," the Swiss peasant went on. With these words, he removed the large, luxuriant mustache he was wearing.

"Sure enough," exclaimed Potts. "But what the devil are you doing here, Jimmy?"

"I'm local color; I'm atmosphere. I work for the company."

"Herding goats?"

"Oh, these goats are props, too; local color. . . . "

" . . . What is this company you're telling me about? Are you an actor?" . . . Jimmy explained to the amazed Potts.

"Switzerland," he said, "is nothing but a fake, an amusement park owned by a very wealthy company. The whole show is put on for the tourist trade—lakes, forests, glaciers, yodelers, peasants, goats, milkmaids, mountains and the rest of it. It's all scenery. . . . It's like the opera."

"The mountains, too, eh?" asked Potts. . . . But how about the avalanches and crevasses?"

"All fake," said Jimmy airily. "If you tumble into a crevasse, you fall on soft snow, and there is a porter at the bottom of every one of them to brush your clothes and ask for your baggage."

"My," said Potts.

If Joe Rucker in "The Adventurer" is trapped within his dreaming, Potts discovers that there is no reality to which he may awaken; reality itself is an illusion.

"The Sun, the Lady, and the Gas Station" employs a similar theme. The tale is made up of a series of separate panels that are related in the common insight they afford. They include a visit to the "Streets of Paris" exhibit at the 1933 Century of Progress Fair in Chicago; a memory of building a boat in a vacant lot; a Beverly Hills dinner party; and a story told there. In each case, the sun exposes the falseness of appearances. At the Century of Progress Fair, the "exhibit looked very badly in the bright sun, very cheap and phony, but then even the real Paris would have probably looked the same way." The boat is built from dream debris, and "looked really horrible. I learned then never to look at junk or machinery when the sun is smiling. Don't even look at people." In the brilliant sunlight, the glittering "Miracle Mile" of Beverly Hills "looked just like the main street of Asbury Park, New Jersey." At the dinner, as the sun shines into the glass-enclosed room, "those of us who were fat looked greasy and soiled, those of us who were thin looked rubbed and faded."

Finally, at the dinner one of the guests tells a story about "an old actress" who wants to sleep with a handsome gas station attendant. In an attempt to restore her faded beauty, she goes to a plastic surgeon, who makes incisions and pours paraffin under those parts of her face that she wants built up, creating a new nose and chin. She arranges to meet the gas station attendant on a day when the sun is particularly hot, and while they are together, talking and drinking, the paraffin in the old actress's nose begins to melt. The gas station man watches in amazement as her chin begins to sag and her face becomes long and pointed; and as she turns into a crone he begins laughing. Once he begins laughing, he finds that he cannot stop. Like "Mr. Potts of Pottstown," the story is a parable, in which external reality is revealed as actual emptiness, providing no arena for effective action. In such a world of sham appearances, the individual can only be thwarted; and in this respect, the story is a preliminary sketch for the dilemma of Lemuel Pitkin in *A Cool Million*.

A Cool Million or, the Dismantling of Lemuel Pitkin is reminiscent at times of two European works in which a young hero's wanderings have the form of an education in pessimism. The first name of West's hero is clearly taken from the name Lemuel Gulliver, and his encounters with irrationality in life have an affinity with those of Swift's hero.[2] But Voltaire's *Candide, or Optimism* is also brought to mind by West's novel, since Lemuel Pitkin, like Voltaire's hero, is a naive youth who leaves his sheltered world to enter the great one, and is subjected to a series of harsh shocks that work against any possible affirmative view of life.[3] Moreover, the three principal characters in *A Cool Million*–Lemuel, Shagpole Whipple, and Betty Prail–have counterparts in *Candide*, in Candide, Pangloss (his mentor), and Cunegonde. They travel about, encounter disaster after disaster, are separated at times (sometimes presuming the others dead), like Voltaire's characters; and *A Cool Million* like *Candide* forms a ceaseless attack on optimistic beliefs.

But the real source for *A Cool Million* is Horatio Alger, Jr., whose popular books for boys offered a formula for success parodied by West. Like Alger's prototypical boys, Lemuel Pitkin is a fatherless lad from the country who is called upon to prove himself. When the local squire threatens foreclosure on the home of his widowed mother, he ventures out into the world to save the house. In the course of his adventures, he confronts "types" corresponding to those in the Alger novels—the Bully, for example, the Sharper, and the Intemperate Spendthrift. West has tailored his characters to the pattern of Alger's two-dimensional ones, and has adjusted his style to Alger's spare, literal prose, which calls attention to suspenseful action—including melodramatic incidents, startling coincidences, and sudden reversals of fortune. Alger's novels are essentially "romances" disguised as realism, celebrations of popular myth, and West's novel is a kind of strange "romance," in which Alger's mythic assumptions are overturned.

A Cool Million is not the first American work to have parodied the Alger books. Stephen Crane in "A Self-Made Man" (1900) and F. Scott Fitzgerald in *The Vegetable* (1922) and "Forging Ahead" (1929) wrote in conscious mockery of Alger's success myth. *The Great Gatsby* itself, in which the young hero had slept "among his Alger books," is an explosion of that myth. But *A Cool Million* is unique in the closeness with which West has reproduced Alger and at the same time parodied him. The degree to which West drew from Alger has now been documented and is quite startling. In 1965 Douglas Shepard published an essay in which he established that West, "without benefit of acknowledgment," quoted directly from two of Alger's novels, *Joe's Luck* and *Andy Grant's Pluck*.[4] Since then, in 1980, Gary Scharnhorst has shown that West appropriated passages from four other Alger novels—*Andy Gordon, Tom Temple's Career, The Erie Train Boy,* and *Ben Bruce*.[5] Scharnhorst has estimated, in fact, that over a fifth of *A Cool Million* was derived from Alger, with only the slightest modification.

How closely West adapted Alger's material is made

clear by Scharnhorst in his citings of many parallel passages, of which a single example may be used to illustrate:

Tom Temple's Career, chapter 8	*A Cool Million*, chapter 3
The next day Tom went on an exploring expedition. He was returning about the middle of the afternoon when he was startled by a young girl's shriek. Turning his head, he saw a terrified figure pursued by a fierce dog. A moment's glance revealed to him that it was Mary Somers.	As he passed a wooded stretch he cut a stout stock with a thick gnarled top. He was twirling this club, . . . when he was startled by a young girl's shriek. Turning his head, he saw a terrified figure pursued by a fierce dog. A moment's glance showed him it was Betty Prail.
She recognized him at the same moment.	Betty recognized him at the same moment.
"Oh, save me, Mr. Temple!" she exclaimed, clasping her hands.	"Oh, save me, Mr. Pitkin!" she exclaimed, clasping her hands.
"I will," said Tom resolutely.	"I will," said Lem resolutely. Armed with the stock he had most fortunately cut, he rushed between the girl and her pursuer and brought the knob down with full force on the dog's head. The attention of the furious animal—a large bulldog—was diverted to his assailant, and with a fierce howl he rushed upon Lem. But our hero was wary and expected the attack. He jumped to one
Tom had been in the woods, when, by good fortune, he had cut a stout stock with a thick, gnarled top, something like the top of a cane. Armed with this weapon, he rushed between Mary and her pursuer, and brought down the knob with full force on the dog's back. The attention of the animal—a large bulldog—was diverted to	

the assailant. With a fierce howl he rushed upon Tom. But our hero was wary and expected the attack. He jumped to one side and brought down the stock with terrible force upon the dog's head. The animal fell, partially stunned, his quivering tongue protruding from his mouth.

side and brought the stick down with great force on the dog's head. The animal fell, partly stunned, his quivering tongue protruding from his mouth.

Significantly, however, the parallel passage just quoted leads to a reversal of the situation in Alger's novel. In Alger, the hero saves the girl in distress, but in West's version, Lem kills the dog only to be confronted by its wayward owner, the bully Tom Baxter, who seizes him and squeezes him senseless. Betty Prail faints and Baxter stands over her "admiring her beauty," his little "pig-like eyes" shining with bestiality. He is last seen "undressing" the girl—whose fate is left to the reader to imagine. At every stage of his adventures, Lem's experiences lead to grotesque misfortune; instead of the providence that shines on Alger's boys, rewarding them for their steadfastness, assisting them through chance meetings with strangers of remarkable decency, a malignant power seems to guide Lem's steps, as he is constantly battered and humiliated.

Lem's story, although complicated, can perhaps be told briefly. At seventeen he leaves his village in rural Vermont to seek his fortune in the world. The local great man, Shagpole Whipple, a former President of the United States and now head of the local bank, lends him thirty dollars at an exorbitant rate of interest, and tells him that he cannot fail if he holds fast to the old-fashioned ideals of enterprise, thrift, and industry. No sooner is he on board the train to New York, however, than his pocket is picked, and he himself, through an error, is arrested, handcuffed, and sentenced to the penitentiary. At the penitentiary all his teeth are pulled out, to "ward off infection"; and when he is eventually given a pardon he boards a train to New York wearing a pair of false teeth. In the city, he heroically prevents an old gentleman and his daughter from being run over by runaway horses; but instead of being thanked (or rewarded, as an Alger hero would be), he is railed at by the rich old gentleman, who believes that he is a careless groom who has let the horses get out of control. Moreover, an injury from a flying stone, incurred in the course of his effort, sends him to the hospital where his right eye is removed.

Penniless, he again meets Shagpole Whipple, whose bank in Ottsville has folded, and is now a soapbox orator in the city, head of the newly formed National Revolutionary Party. Innocently, Lem joins him for what turns out to be more bizarre adventures. One incident brings him into contact again with Betty Prail, who had been spirited away by white slavers and is now an unwilling prostitute in the "house" of the Chinese Wu Fong. In attempting to rescue her, Lem himself barely escapes being forced into male prostitution, and his protest to the police about the notorious house results in his being thrown into jail. When he is released, he is fortuitously reunited with Betty and Whipple, and they, together with Whipple's American Indian follower Jake Raven, board a transcontinental train for the West Coast. During a brief stopover in Chicago, Lem is separated from the others, abducted by agents of the Third International, and involved in an automobile accident that claims his left thumb.

Miraculously, he is able to rejoin the others before the train leaves, and the group safely reaches its California destination. They travel by horseback into the high Sierras to dig for gold in the mine of an abandoned camp, but before long a sinister Missourian appears, and violence quickly ensues. Emerging from the mine the next day, Lem hears a scream, rushes to the cabin, near which he finds Jake Raven shot in the chest, and enters the cabin with ax in hand as the Missourian is about to rape Betty. Rushing to her rescue, Lem steps into a bear trap placed in his path by the Missourian; and while he is thus impaled, Betty is again sexually victimized. Worse, when Jake Raven crawls to a nearby Indian reservation declaring the treachery of a white man before he faints, the tribe rises in revolt, and upon reaching the cabin chief Satinpenny takes Lem's scalp. When Whipple finally returns to the camp, he carries Lem to a nearby hospital, where his leg is amputated at the knee.

Now, with the loss of his teeth, an eye, a thumb, a leg, and his scalp, Lem is exhibited by Whipple in a traveling show called the "Chamber of American Horrors." When the troupe reaches the South, a riot occurs, and Lem escaping with his life begs a long series of rides back to New York. In the city, he joins the great army of the unemployed, living in a piano crate on the shore of Central Park Lake until an employment agency finds him work as a "stooge" with a vaudeville act. On stage Riley and Robbins pommel him until his glass eye pops out and his toupee tumbles off. After further clubbing his wooden leg is knocked into the audience to the delighted guffaws of the crowd. It is on this stage that he is shot to death by an agent of the Third International, practically his last words being, "I am a clown." In an epilogue that leaps forward in time, Whipple's revolutionary party has seized power, and Lem is honored as a martyr. Betty Prail and old Mrs. Pitkin join Whipple on the reviewing stand, as Whipple's storm troops pass by, and the crowd joins in singing "The Lemuel Pitkin Song."

Particularly in comparison with *Miss Lonelyhearts*, *A Cool Million* seems surprisingly crude and rambling. It develops in a series of episodes, the humor of which is at times nearly as heavy-handed as the fulsome lyrics of "The Lemuel Pitkin Song." Almost all of West's critics have regarded *A Cool Million* as the slightest of West's novels, of interest today as an experiment in Depression-period black humor. Although it is a political allegory and a satire of American life, it is primarily a grotesque comedy, as Jay Martin has noted in comparing the work to Poe's bizarre tale "The Man Who Was Used Up."[6] Despite its flaws, however, *A Cool Million* does have a certain resonance as a Depression fable that is both comic and horrifying.

Its fable quality begins in the heartland of New England, in rural Vermont, where the humble Pitkin home, both within and without, is the essence of plainspun American Colonial. The American colonial experience is immediately suggested by it, but even in the opening chapter, this heritage has become an anachronistic illusion. The house is mortgaged to Squire Bird, who threatens foreclosure in order to sell the property to Asa Goldstein, a New York merchant who deals in exterior and interior decoration. He will, in fact, dismantle the house and reassemble it in the window of his establishment on Fifth Avenue; and it will be sold off to people for whom it will be intrinsically meaningless—window dressing transferred to their anonymous homes. The rudimentary motive of behavior in Ottsville is the acquisition of wealth, and it is for monetary gain that Squire Bird, the wealthiest man of the area, and his agent Mr. Slemp, the rich village lawyer, act together to sell Lem's heritage.

In seeking assistance, Lem applies to Shagpole Whipple, the ex-President of the United States modeled in part on Calvin Coolidge, the flinty Vermonter whose administration allied itself with American business interests. Instead of helping him, Whipple offers Lem "mythic" advice about opportunity in America for a young man willing to make his own way. A skinflint, he lends Lem thirty dollars so that he may begin his rite of passage into maturity and success, charging a usurious rate of interest, with the prospect of taking possession, in almost certain default of the loan, of the Pitkin cow, worth a hundred dollars and the sole source of the widow's milk and cheese. It is entirely appropriate that Whipple's home should also be his place of business (his bank occupying the whole of its first floor), since his life consists of little more than a denial of personal pleasure for the sake of getting on in the world. Even his den, his inner sanctum located in the garage, testifies to his drably spartan shrewdness and self-serving "patriotism." Furnished with a cracker barrel, pot-bellied stove, and spittoon, it has on one of its walls a picture of Abraham Lincoln, the great "emancipator" with whom Whipple "silently communes." Every evening at sunset, Whipple lowers the American flag that flies over the garage, crying "All Hail Old Glory" as he tenderly gathers the bunting up in his arms. Indeed, the name "Shagpole," conferred on him by the citizenry, is a coarse-grained version of "flagpole" (as "Whipple" is a version of "whip"). Whipple becomes Lem's spiritual father, sending him forth into the world; but it is apparent even early in the work that he is also Lem's deceiver.

Ottsville itself is a travesty of the American colonial past, an exposure of the American heritage as a sour joke. It is significantly situated on the Rat River, and its inhabitants are notably mean-spirited and perverse. When Betty Prail (whose last name suggests both "frail" and a "pail" to be unfeelingly kicked about) is left an orphan at an early age, she is sent to the county orphanage until she is fourteen, then becomes a maid of all work for lawyer Slemp. Betty is, as it happens, an attractive girl, and arouses the jealousy of Slemp's shrewish wife and two ugly daughters, who see to it that, like Cinderella, she is dressed in the homeliest garb. Moreover, Slemp, although a deacon in the church, beats her "regularly and enthusiastically." Since she is in her late teens at this time, his spankings "on her bare behind with his bare hand" have glaringly sexual overtones—a measure of the repression and hypocrisy to be found in Ottsville.

What one also finds in Ottsville is depraved animality. The scene in which Tom Baxter rapes Betty while she is unconscious is not the first of her sexual victimizations in the village. Earlier, as a child, she had been raped, also while unconscious, by Baxter's father, in what is apparently a father-son tradition. The scene in which this occurs forms one of the more vivid moments in the novel. While the Prail house burns, the members of the fire company are seen drinking applejack, playing checkers, and telling dirty stories; and when they respond to the fire they are dead drunk. Instead of attempting to quell the blaze, they proceed to loot the house, and little Betty, "dressed only in a cotton nightgown," is lured into a woodshed by fire chief Baxter to be raped.

If Ottsville is corrupt at its core, the world without is equally discouraging. Pickpockets and swindlers circulate on trains and in the public parks and streets of the city, and policemen have a goonlike mentality. It is typical of Lem's experience that after reporting Wu Fong's house of prostitution to a policeman he should be clubbed by him, thrown into jail, and fleeced by a shyster lawyer for services never rendered. The upholders of the law and those who violate it are hardly distinguishable in their meanness and mutual assault on innocence. As Lem, the male naif, is repeatedly beaten and physically disfigured, so Betty Prail, the female innocent, is endlessly raped.

The paths of Lem and Betty cross in New York's Chinatown, where Betty has been impressed into a life of prostitution, a sequence that suggests a house of mirrors in its emphasis on illusion. Wu Fong's establishment is a kind of reproduction (an importation from Europe) of a famous house of ill fame in the Rue Chabanis in Paris, known as the "House of All Nations." His girls are kept in suites having the decor of the countries they are supposed to represent, and they themselves are dressed appropriately. The suite of the Spanish girl, for example, contains a grand piano with a fancy shawl gracefully draped over it, and on one wall a tiny balcony has been painted "by a poor but consummate artist." Betty is confined in the colonial suite, which contains hooked rugs, antimacassars, and ships in bottles; and she wears an elaborate eighteenth-century costume and hairdo, with puff-combs on each side of her face. In a Westian touch, her first client is "a pockmarked Armenian rug merchant from Malta." Thereafter she is visited by a procession of "Orientals, Slavs, Latins, Celts, and Semites" who suggest the opened gates of immigration in America.

Wu Fong is depicted in the work as a shrewd businessman. He is protected by the police, and his brothel is furnished by the eminently respectable Asa Goldstein, dealer in decoration and veneers to an anonymous public. A prosperous entrepreneur, Wu Fong knows how to merchandise, to adapt his business to the latest trends. When Hearst's "Buy America" campaign works up patriotic fervor, for example, he converts his brothel into an "All American" house, with girls consigned to suites in the style of their indigenous regions. Mary Judkins, spirited away from Arkansas, is in a suite with real dirt on its floors and is dressed in homespun. Princess Roan Fawn, from an Oklahoma Indian Reservation, occupies a suite in which the walls have been papered with birch bark to make it look like a wigwam, and she does business on the floor, where she lies naked under a bull's-eye blanket. The various regions of the country have been extracted in the form of female victims of commercial lust—women who are plundered, used, and soiled. Later the novel reaches out across the continent to the gold fields of California, where the Pike County man is encountered, a gunslinging braggart who might have stepped out of the pages of Mark Twain, and the episode ends in violence and heedless lust as he ravishes Betty in the cabin. The spoliation of the country, from New England to California, and in every region lying between, is projected in terms of what in West often seems the uncleanest of things—sexuality.

The spoliation theme is announced overtly late in the work when Lem and Whipple join a traveling troupe that exhibits a "Chamber of American Horrors/Animate and Inanimate Hideosities." The animate part of the exhibition is called "The Pageant of America or A Curse on Columbus," and consists of short sketches in which Quakers are shown being branded, Indians brutalized and cheated, Negroes sold, and children "sweated to death." But the stranger part deals with the inanimate—a corruption of nature by the commercial uses to which it is put. Here such artifacts are displayed as paper grained to look like wood, and a Hercules "wearing a small, compact truss." In the center of the principal salon is "a gigantic hemorrhoid that was lit from within by electric lights. To give the effect of throbbing pain, these lights went on and off." The throbbing pain might almost be said to be Lem's, as he is buffeted about in a mercilessly irrational world.

A Cool Million is anticipated in some respects by *Miss Lonelyhearts*. The crowd in the earlier novel that moves with "dreamlike violence" through the streets of the South Bronx slums, with the implied threat of unleashing its anger upon the social order, has been reimagined in *A Cool Million* as a suppressed violence on a national scale. An important difference between the two works is that *A Cool Million* addresses itself much more directly and fully to Depression conditions. The social and economic system by the time of *A Cool Million* has reached a point of breakdown. The police are brutal and cynical, justice cannot be found, there is no communication between people, the innocent and trusting are trampled underfoot. The implication of a collapsing social and moral order can be noticed in a number of novels that appeared in 1934, when *A Cool Million* was published and the Depression was at its height. The sense of a house collapsing upon itself is felt at the end of James T. Farrell's *Studs Lonigan* trilogy, and a mood of collapsing values is pervasive in Fitzgerald's *Tender Is the Night*; but West goes a step further to envision an actual breakdown, an apocalyptic revolution in the country.

West's vision of a radical breakdown of the social order and the coming to power of a new, even more repressive regime was clearly influenced by the rise to power of the Nazis in Germany in 1933, when *A Cool Million* was conceived. Nathan "Shagpole" Whipple, a patriot of the Far Right, is evoked as a Yankee Hitler, a leader who feels called upon to save the republic from the "disease of sophistication," from alien influences (particularly of international Jewish bankers and Soviet Marxists) that have supposedly corrupted native values. Whipple's "leather shirts" are a version of Hitler's "black shirts," and at the end his "storm troops" pass in review along Fifth Avenue, the Under der Linden of New York.

But in imagining his fable of the coming to power of American fascism, West also drew upon American sources. The hue and cry for a return to an earlier national "purity" (comparable in kind to the obsession with restoring national and ethnic purity in Germany) was witnessed in Depression America in a variety of ways: in the rise of populist demagogues like Huey Long; the proto-Nazi, Jew-baiting radio broadcasts of Father Coughlin; and the "patriotic" yellow journalism of William Randolph Hearst. Hearst is alluded to specifically in the novel, and Robert I. Edenbaum, in his article on *A*

Cool Million,[7] has called attention to Hearst as providing an "ideological framework" for Whipple's crusade for a restoration of "Americanism." In the 1930s, through the newspapers he controlled, Hearst waged a continual war on intellectuals and the importation of foreign ideas; he opposed strikes as "an importation from Russia," as well as big bankers and Wall Street; and at times his attitudes brought him close to an open admiration of European fascism. His Right Wing ideology and concern with a preservation of "Americanism" lend credence to Whipple, whose party insignias are the New England squirrel rifle and the frontier coonskin cap.

Foreign agents appear at various times in the novel with the effect of a comically sinister cartoon (another instance of West's use of the comic strip in his fiction). The fat man in a Chesterfield overcoat, known as Operative 6385XM, is, contradictorily, both an agent for international Jewish bankers and for the Communist Party. He orders thugs to bash heads and break up Whipple's first political rally in New York, and he has Lem kidnaped during his stayover in Chicago. Later he is revealed as the power behind the "Chamber of American Horrors," and at the end he is Lem's assassin. His ominous appearances in the novel have the effect of objectifying Whipple's worst fears. Drawn in shadowy and simplistic outline, Operative 6385XM is a bugaboo in the mind of Whipple and his followers, and reinforces the sense that their political ideas are shadowy and simplistic also.

Despite West's farcical treatment, Whipple's rise to power has a certain plausibility, since he understands and reflects the public mind. His jingoism and distrust of alien influences are part of American mass consciousness, particularly that of the lower middle class, from which his support comes. This stratum of society, later studied by Richard Hofstadter in *Anti-Intellectualism in American Life* (1963), would certainly have been in tune with

Whipple's ideology, which emphasizes the spoliation of American ideals from "without." R. W. B. Lewis has commented on *A Cool Million* in this regard as a work of considerable insight, calling it "this country's most vigorous narrative vision of the political apocalypse."[8] Although Lewis's claim for the novel seems considerably exaggerated, one does feel, in reading the work, that Whipple's coming to power in the midst of Depression disillusionment is just possible, that if an overthrow of the government were to occur under such conditions, it would no doubt be led by a paternalistic figure as disarmingly amiable and ambitious, as cannily manipulative and fraudulent as Shagpole Whipple.

An odd feature of *A Cool Million* is that many of its male characters have been given Hebraic or Old Testament first names. Whipple's given name is Nathan; Squire Bird's is Joshua; warden Purdy's name is Ezekiel; district attorney Barnes's is Elisha; bank president Underwood's is Levi. Even the American Indian Israel Satinpenny has a Hebraic first name. What West seems to have in mind is an implied analogy with the tribes of Israel, a people whose lofty covenant with God has been breached, their high heritage despoiled, just as the American Dream has been despoiled in the Depression. In their frustration, the Israelites nurture the idea, religious in intensity, of vindication, of throwing off a foreign yoke, of restoring the promised land, of establishing the New Jerusalem. And West's characters, in their frustration at the failure of the American Dream, harbor a great yearning to vindicate that dream, even though in West's terms it had never been real in the first place.

It should be noted that Whipple's Revolutionary Party first begins to take hold when, traveling with the "Chamber of American Horrors," he visits the Southern Bible Belt. His speech extolling the earlier pristine America takes place in a town ironically named Beulah,

after the land of heavenly joy described by John Bunyan
in *The Pilgrim's Progress*. The speech soon unleashes the
ugliest passions in the crowd, which vents its anger upon
"alien" scapegoats. The mob marches on the opera house
to put a rope around the neck of the Indian Jake Raven,
"because of his dark complexion." Barricades are thrown
up in the streets, and the heads of blacks are paraded on
poles. A Jewish drummer is crucified, "nailed to the door
of his hotel room," and the housekeeper of the local
Catholic priest is raped. The episode in Beulah, although
it ends in tumult, provides the first big push of the wave
that sweeps Whipple to power. His accession to power is
deeply ironic, for his regime makes the meanness,
avarice, and hypocrisy of Ottsville a venerated national
ideal. The cream of the jest is that while Lem perishes,
Whipple succeeds even beyond the dreams of an Alger
hero. Through his manipulative skills, he advances himself and fulfills the American dream. His success, at the
same time, reveals how empty that dream is.

West's fable is reinforced by an inner fable that centers
on the relationship of Whipple and Lem. Whipple is, first
of all, Lem's guide and initiator into experience. When
Lem comes to him for help, Whipple offers a vision:
" 'America,' he said with great seriousness, 'is the land of
opportunity. She takes care of the honest and industrious
and never fails them as long as they are both. This is not a
matter of opinion, it is one of faith.' " Armed with this
faith, Lem leaves Whipple only to be rudely confronted
by Tom Baxter, whose physical violence upon him and
sexual violence upon Betty begin a pattern that runs
through the novel. Yet Lem continues to be called upon
by Whipple to keep faith. In New York he lays his hand
on Lem's shoulder, like a priest annointing an acolyte,
and asks him to join his cause. Many tricksters appear in
the work—more even than in Melville's *The Confidence
Man*—and in one way or another they comment on Whip-

ple. One of them is the old-style American poet Sylvanus
Snodgrass, who has the free-flowing mane of hair and the
high, broad forehead of nineteenth-century American
orators. There is something of Webster in his appearance,
and his poetic gift has an eminently patriotic cast. Having
witnessed Lem's courageous act in preventing an old
gentleman and his daughter from being run over by bolt-
ing carriage horses, Snodgrass eulogizes him in public,
declaring that national monuments should be raised to
him throughout the land, while his agents use the occasion to pick the crowd's pockets. Snodgrass's appearance
underscores the fraudulence of Whipple, whose
memorialization of Lem as a party martyr is to be self-
serving.

But Whipple is implied to be more than a treacherous
guide. Lem is a fatherless boy, while Whipple is distinctly
a father figure as an ex-President, and, in effect, he
becomes Lem's father. This implication is strengthened
through associations of naming. Lem's widowed mother
is named Sarah, who, in the Old Testament, was the wife
of Abraham, the great patriarch and father figure.[9] In his
devotion to a Godly ideal, Abraham stands ready to sacrifice his own son Isaac; and in *A Cool Million* Whipple
plays an analogous role. He is pointedly identified with
another Abraham, Abraham Lincoln, a prophet of democ-
racy; and by the end Lem is sacrificed on the altar of his
beliefs.

R. W. B. Lewis has remarked that West "is not himself implicated in that which he satirizes"[10] in *A Cool
Million*, as he had been earlier in *Miss Lonelyhearts*, and
in doing so misses an entire dimension of the novel. Just
before *A Cool Million* was written, West's own father,
Max Weinstein, had died in reduced circumstances.
Although there were no personal resemblances between
Max Weinstein and Whipple, he was, nevertheless, a
believer in the American Dream. An immigrant, he had

risen to success in America, and had adopted its ideals. Indeed, one of his earliest gifts to his son was a set of the Alger books. How ironic then that Max Weinstein should have been wiped out by the Depression, should have lived to see the ideals he had adopted betrayed. The bitterness at the core of *A Cool Million* can surely be traced to West's own sense of betrayal by a system in which his father had brought him up to believe. At the very time when West was writing *A Cool Million*, he could find no way to support himself, and his continued existence as a novelist was gravely in doubt. West could only too easily conceive his father's legacy to him as a "betrayal," and himself as a victim, like Lem, who is deceived and dismembered—on a sexual level, castrated. It could even be said that the novel enacts a ritualistic castration of the son by the father.

In viewing *A Cool Million* purely as political satire, Lewis also overlooks the romance-fable dimension that is at the heart of the book. Martin comes closer to the essence of the work when he refers to Poe and Melville, Kafka and Gogol, as its forebears in "grotesque comedy"; but another antecedent, natively American and more recent, is F. Scott Fitzgerald in his story "The Diamond as Big as the Ritz" (1922). "The Diamond as Big as the Ritz," like *A Cool Million*, is a bizarre fable that is concerned with the American Dream. The events it records take place in a middle region between realism and extravagant fantasy. Its hero is a naive American youth, like Lem, who has been instructed by an elder figure, his father in fact, that if he keeps faith with the ideals espoused by his native town of Hades he cannot fail to find success and happiness. He journeys out into the world, again like Lem, to make disturbing recognitions, one of which is that his father is not all he has seemed and that he has betrayed him.

The idea of the father as betrayer is compounded by

the hero's nightmarish meeting with Braddock Washington, who has the lineage and name of the father of the republic. Washington lives in garish splendor, designed by Hollywood film people who can neither read nor write, atop a hideaway mountain that is a huge solid diamond. His existence is the fulfillment of the American Dream, and consists of avarice beyond conception and the deepest callousness to every humane value. The detonation of the mountain near the end signals the explosion of the dream in which the hero, John Unger, has been brought up to believe; and at the end Unger is alone and bitterly disillusioned. *A Cool Million*, too, illustrates the spuriousness of national myth, and is an explosion of that myth. There are important differences between Fitzgerald's and West's heroes, but they are alike as representative figures whose deception is to be understood in the context of collective dreaming of the country. In both works, the dream and the horror of estrangement that underlies it are brought very close together; and the stories read like dreams that are partly comic and altogether grotesque.

One difference between them is that "A Diamond as Big as the Ritz" moves toward its revelation of the falseness of the dream with mounting suspense, whereas in *A Cool Million* the fraudulence of the dream is known from the start, and one reads on primarily to see what further tortures Lem will have to undergo. The loose structure of *A Cool Million* deprives it of the intense dramatic focus that had been West's strength in *Miss Lonelyhearts*, and is related to the difference in attitude toward their common subject of Fitzgerald and West. In Fitzgerald, the betrayal of the American Dream is made to seem especially, even poignantly, acute because Fitzgerald so deeply believes in that which he repudiates. One feels in *A Cool Million*, on the other hand, that although West may feel the betrayal sharply he has never been a great believer. West is at too great a distance from his characters, who are invariably two-dimensional, and Lem himself fails to engage the reader deeply, not only because he is simple but also because he cannot learn from his experience. He is not merely dismembered but, to use West's word, "dismantled," like a piece of machinery, the absolute victim of a dehumanized world; and one might be able to pity him were he not so passive. "I'm innocent," Lem cries desperately in his jail cell, and the crooked lawyer who is supposed to represent him answers, "So was Christ . . . and they nailed him." Can any reader possibly miss the implication that Lem is the Lamb of Innocence martyred by the world?

A Cool Million employs the theater motif that had appeared earlier in *Balso Snell* and *Miss Lonelyhearts*, but in this version it takes the form of the popular theater of slapstick and farce. In "Mr. Potts of Pottstown" and "The Sun, the Lady, and the Gas Station," West had posited an external world that was wholly without meaning, in which even the Swiss Alps are a commercial deception; and in *A Cool Million* he incorporates this idea in his envisioning of a cardboard American world devoid of genuine values and dominated by the whorehouse and the vaudeville stage. West's vaudeville is only intermittently successful. At its weakest, it lends itself to nitwit humor—seen, for example, in chief Satinpenny's having been educated at Harvard. Satinpenny's speech to the reservation Indians about the impending collapse of the American system, in which he refers to Spengler and Valéry, is heavy-handed and simply fails to come off.

At times, too, sexual undercurrents that move through the work complicate the reader's response. Stanley Edgar Hyman refers to the scene in Wu Fong's brothel when Lem is confronted by the lisping Maharajah Kanurani, "whose tastes were notorious," as perhaps the worst instance of West's "salacious smirking." The scene, however, is related to larger sexual patterns, of a sadomasochistic nature, that appear in the work. One feels, for example, that Betty Prail's seemingly endless sexual degradation is misogynistically gloated over by West, actually enjoyed. As a counterpart to this, one has the masochism of Lem's interminable "punishment," and the hint of repressed homosexuality. A notable feature of Lem is that he never at any time has a sexual experience, and is more virginal than Betty. He is so passive that one is apt to wonder what is wrong with him. His single personal encounter with real sexual experience occurs when he is held in the whorehouse for the Maharajah Kanurani, a sodomist whose last name is an amalgam of "can" and "urani." The maharajah's presence in the novel suggests that Lem's lack of sexual response to women may involve a homosexual temptation that he has not wholly faced, and which in the whorehouse scene is confronted only to be smirked away.

A Cool Million is an extremely odd work that fails to come off, yet is at times quite insightful and contains some brilliant moments. One of its most memorable scenes is the penultimate sequence in which Lem appears on the vaudeville stage with the comedy team of Riley and Robbins. All the characters in the novel act out "roles," which are ultimately meaningless because external reality itself provides no basis for coherence in their lives. In a sense, they invent a reality in the roles they assume. Whipple, for instance, constructs a reality from illusion, and he eventually enforces this illusion upon others. Most of all, Lem is bound by the role he plays as an Alger hero in reverse, and he is not free to participate in life other than as a mute victim. His suffering is implied in his name Pitkin, which stresses his kinship with the pit, that is, the pit of hell. The vaudeville stage, where the serious is deflated, the pretension of meaning derided by guffaws, is the perfect place for Lem's last appearance in the work.

A "stooge" of the vaudeville team, he is clubbed on stage with a rolled-up newspaper that recalls the instrument with which Fay Doyle beat her crippled husband in *Miss Lonelyhearts*. With a similar implication, the newspaper club is a symbol of the culture itself, its vapidity and vulgarization of nature and emotion that defeat reason and render life unintelligible. "I am a clown," Lem steps forward to announce to the audience near the end, "but there are times when even clowns must grow serious." At this moment, as he attempts to step out of his role, to become fully dimensional as a human being, his life is extinguished by a bullet.

In this finely achieved moment, *A Cool Million* rises to its real climax as absurdist theater. Friend and foe alike, Whipple and Operative 6385XM, in their opposition and struggle for power, are unable to create a "reality" that offers escape from despair. In the vaudeville theater these ideologues meet, in effect, to reveal that there is no political solution to Lem's dilemma. There is no solution at all. The agony implied in Lem's inability to break through into "life" is ultimately what connects *A Cool Million* with *Balso Snell* and *Miss Lonelyhearts*; and it looks ahead to *The Day of the Locust*, in which Tod Hackett will attempt to find order in the nightmarish fragmentation of Hollywood. The vaudeville of apocalypse in *A Cool Million* is, in a sense, a dress rehearsal for the apocalypse of West's last novel, in which the dream life of the masses erupts into orgiastic violence, and the work, like a classic horror story, ends with a scream.

5

The Day of the Locust:
Absurdism in Hollywood

When West returned to Hollywood in the mid-thirties, he was already considering a novel about the film capital, but his conception of *The Day of the Locust* took shape only very slowly. A vignette entitled "Bird and Bottle,"[1] in which Earle Schoop appears, and which was later included in *The Day of the Locust*, was published in late 1936, and is the first indication that the novel was under way. A first draft of the novel was accepted by Bennett Cerf for Random House in May 1938, and, following extensive revision, the book was published in the spring of 1939.

West did not find his special subject matter, or the form in which to cast it, immediately. At an early point, he entertained several different ideas for the novel—before discarding them entirely. One was a "ship of fools" conception, suggested by a newspaper story about a boat called *The Wanderer*, which returned from an around-the-world pleasure cruise to become involved in a sordid, café-society scandal when it docked at a California harbor. West's pleasure boat was to have been chartered by a group of grotesques—including movie cowboys, prosti-tutes, a gigantic lesbian, and a family of Eskimos; and the cruise was to have ended in catastrophe, including multiple murders. At times he thought of making the yacht an offshore speakeasy and gambling ship, but in the end he abandoned the idea, while retaining its motif of violence and death, and a few of the character types. Earle Schoop, the cowboy extra in films, and the Gingos, the Eskimos living in Hollywood, made their first, tentative appearance in this early, fragmentary version.

Another early notion for the novel dealt with a boarding house in Hollywood occupied by a group of out-of-work people marginally connected with films. A central figure was an old vaudevillian, "a bedraggled harlequin," his daughter, and other members of his circle. Robert M. Coates, with whom West discussed this conception, has written that the characters would be involved in "a sort of endless double-take, people clowning at funerals, pretending to be sad at weddings, etc., in short, acting endlessly."[2] Crude as this notion was, one can see how West refined it in his conception of Harry Greener, the clown who cannot step out of his role, and the other marginal show business people who live at the San Bernardino Arms.

Another idea that eventually entered into the composition of the novel occurred to West when he was living at Erwinna, and had not yet left for Hollywood. He told an Erwinna friend of his sense of a character "who was conscious of her hands, her hands seemed to her enormous—and at times as though they had nothing to do with the rest of her, she was ashamed of them and frightened by them." This conceit was brought brilliantly to life in West's portrayal not of a woman but of a man, the hapless, small-town bookkeeper Homer Simpson. Still other characters and details in *The Day of the Locust* came from West's own experience in Hollywood. His apartment building on North Ivar Street supplied the details for the Ivar Street apartment house where Tod lives at the opening of the novel; and the dwarf who sold newspapers on the corner inspired the character of Abe Kusich. Even Audrey Jennings's call house and the Cinderella bar were suggested by actual places in Los Angeles that West knew personally. Moreover, with his friend Stanley Rose, West went to boxing matches at the American Legion Arena and to cockfights held illegally in the Hollywood hills and at Pismo Beach, and all of these experiences made him an expert witness of the Los Angeles-Hollywood scene, and are vital to the novel.

What is surprising about the composition of *The Day of the Locust* is that Tod Hackett emerged as the novel's hero only in the final draft.[3] In the early version, the central figure and first-person narrator was Claude Estee. By April 1938, after several revisions, West recast the novel in the third person, and reduced Estee to a peripheral figure, while expanding upon the role played by Tod. At this stage, West had also included material from his ship-of-fools conception that was later eliminated. One episode, for instance, included a glimpse of a "sloppy old nude who drools over her 'cello,' kissing its neck and making it groan in reply," a scene that introduced Abe Kusich. Present also was Mrs. Schwartzen, a seven-foot lesbian who needs to shave every day, and who, in Audrey Jennings's call house, accosts one of the girls. Mrs. Schwartzen was retained in the final version, but although mannish she is not of gigantic stature and her lesbian implications are suppressed. What was enlarged upon particularly in the revisions was Tod's artistlike perceptions of his surroundings—the textures, colors, and tactile qualities of things as they would appeal to the "painter's eye." West's allusions to painters of the past, particularly to the painters of "Decay and Mystery," appeared only in this final draft.

As submitted to Random House, the novel was entitled *The Cheated*, and West later considered using other titles (such as *The Wroth to Come*), until settling upon *The Day of the Locust*, a title that may have been suggested by Gilbert Seldes's book on the Depression, *The Years of the Locust* (1932). West's title, in any case, seems apt in its implication of a day of wrath and apocalypse, as prophesied in the Bible. More specifically, the title appears to come from the Book of Exodus (10:1–11), in the passage where Moses and Aaron warn Pharaoh that unless the Hebrews are allowed to worship Yahweh, the Lord "shall cover the face of the earth" with locusts, which will reduce the land to utter waste. The prophets are driven from Pharaoh's presence, and thereafter "the Lord brought an east wind upon the land all day, and all that night; and when it was moving, the east wind brought the locusts [which] covered the face of the whole earth . . . and there remained not any green thing in the trees, or in the herbs of the field, through all the land of Egypt."[4]

The Day of the Locust begins with the sound of thundering hoofs, as a sound-stage army is scattered in defeat and confusion. The fleeing army resembles a mob, and its chaos is a foreshadowing, at the very opening, of the novel's final scene. But it also introduces the theme of masquerade that quickly involves all of the novel's characters. Tod Hackett leaves the film studio after work, for instance, to notice a crowd of people on Vine Street who are costumed like actors. A fat woman wearing a yachting cap has been shopping, not boating, and a girl in slacks and sneakers with a bandanna around her head has just left a switchboard, not a tennis court. They are all illusionists.

Los Angeles, as West has imagined it, conditions the mind to accept the fantastic as normal. Even nature contributes to an unsettling effect of unreality. The city's sunsets, with a theatrical violet lighting effect, "like a Neon tube," make the ugly hills in the distance seem "almost beautiful." In one of the many small, perfectly visualized effects in the novel, Tod looks out his office window to notice eucalyptus foliage that stirs in a light breeze, so that the narrow leaves show first their green side, then their silver one—an impression like that of an optical illusion. The Los Angeles architecture, moreover, adds to the pervasive effect of a theatrical identity rather than a real one. On the La Huerta Road, a house resembles a miniature Rhine castle, with tarpaper turrets containing slits for archers' bows; but what is remarkable about the building is that, in the context of its surroundings, it should seem "normal." All along the slopes of the canyon, houses are styled as Samoan huts, Tudor cottages, Swiss chalets, and Egyptian temples.

The cottage rented by Homer Simpson is a masterpiece of the eclectic and incongruous. With its thatched roof and big chimney, it has been built in a style called "Irish." Yet its living room—which has silk armorial banners in red and gold on its walls, and a big galleon on the mantlepiece—is "Spanish," and its two bedrooms are in the "New England" style. The "New England" bedrooms, in fact, are exact duplicates, with everything in them machine-made. Actually, the entire house is machine-made. Its front door is made of gumwood painted to look like oak, and its hinges are carefully stamped to appear hand-forged. The thatching is not really straw, but "heavy fireproof colored and ribbed to look like straw." The cottage, which might have been displayed in the "Chamber of American Horrors," is incoherent; and it is, fittingly, the setting of several harrowing scenes and of Homer's final breakdown.

Almost all of the characters in *The Day of the Locust* are middle or less-than-middle class; most are displaced people who can hardly remember where they once came from, and many are unemployed. An exception is Claude Estee, a successful screenwriter whose house is viewed early in the work. What is striking about the house is that it has the same quality of illusion as the dwellings of the middle-class characters. It is a big house: an exact repro-

duction of the old Dupuy mansion near Biloxi, Mississippi. When Tod appears at the house, he is greeted by
Estee who "poses" for a moment as a pot-bellied Southern colonel, although he is actually a thin man with narrow shoulders and (a favorite phrase of West's) "rubbed
features." He calls "Here, you black rascal! A mint
julep," and a moment later a Chinese servant brings a
scotch and soda. Estee's *Gone With the Wind* house
means nothing, implies his lack of relation to the past or
to a stable tradition of any kind.

At Estee's gathering, the male guests from the studios
engage in "shop talk," chiefly about the need to give the
film "racket" a respectable front, as Rockefeller had done
for his oil empire by establishing a philanthropic founda-
tion. A female guest, Joan Schwartzen, is described startlingly as having "a pretty, eighteen-year-old face and a
thirty-five-year-old neck that was veined and sinewy,"
and she is interested in "smut." She is also fascinated by
the Estees' swimming pool, which appears to contain a
dead horse, its belly hideously bloated and distended, its
mouth—from which lolls a "heavy, black tongue"—set in
"an agonized grin." But it is actually a studio mock-up,
no more real than anything else at the house. When a
woman reminds Mrs. Schwartzen that the horse, after all,
is not real, she exclaims: "You're just like that mean Mr.
Hackett. You just won't let me cherish my illusions."
Later, Estee and his guests attend a private showing of a
prurient film at another house in the city, the call house of
Audrey Jennings, a former film star who, thrown out of
work by talking pictures, has become successful as a
madam for polite society. She permits her girls to service
only men of wealth and position, "not to say taste and
discretion," and her taste and culture seem flawless. Her
good taste, however, is merely a veneer for her selling of
sex, an illusion of transcendence; and in this respect, West
has made her a complementary figure to Estee, the film
writer.

A person of small importance at the studios, Tod lives at the opening of the novel at the San Bernardino Arms apartment house, called the "San Berdoo." Earlier he had lived at a shabby hotel on Ivar Street having a fairytale name,' the Chateau Mirabella. The hotel had been occupied by so many prostitutes that in the morning its hallways reeked of sexual odors; and they, too, with their "managers, trainers, and advance agents," belong to the theater motif of the novel. It is at the Chateau Mirabella that Tod first meets Abe Kusich, the pugnacious dwarf with a slightly hydrocephalic head, who also has show business affiliations, since he is a racetrack tout whose tips on horses are a huckstering of romantic dreams. He even has cards printed up on which endorsements are quoted as if they were taken from reviews he had received in the press.

Abe persuades Tod to move to the San Berdoo, where he himself lives, together with others on the fringes of show business. The building has a façade of a bright mustard color, with windows framed by pink Moorish columns, supporting turnip-shaped lintels; and it gives an impression of garish romance. The reality beneath the façade, however, is that the building is as characterless as Homer's Irish cottage, and is a haven for failures, people sustained by some expectation of success in the future or by memory of past success romanticized out of all relation to reality. Anna and Annabelle Lee, who live there, and take their parody names from Poe's famous ballad of the mystical beauty of a young girl, were years before a youthful sister act on the vaudeville stage, and have only this meager memory to furnish them with an identity. The Gingos, a family of performing Eskimos from Point Barrow no more belong in Hollywood than they do anywhere else, and are merely culturally uprooted exiles who are committed to a fantasy existence.

Other characters have no homes at all. Earle Schoop, an occasional extra in westerns and Vine Street loafer, leads a vagrant's existence. At one point he lives in the garage of Homer's cottage, but it is hardly a home; he doesn't even belong there, and before long he is forced to leave. Nor does he have any real connection with the cowboy's life as it was once lived. Lacking genuine identity, he stands for hours like a studio prop before a saddlery shop window displaying sharp spurs and other "torture instruments," and engages in small talk with other extras, which is as banal and bromidic as their lives are pointless. His lack of identity is implied in his featureless face and in his legs which are "so straight that his dungarees . . . hung down without a wrinkle, as though they were empty." Another idler before the saddlery shop, an American Indian who seems as homeless as Earle, sells what are supposed to be objects of his culture but are actually junk. He is described grotesquely: the inside of his mouth is "black," his teeth are "broken" and "orange." At one point he is called "Chief Kiss-My-Towkus," making his life seem like a vulgar vaudeville jest, an association reinforced by his use of the phrase "Vas you dere, Sharley?," the tag line of a famous vaudeville team that had flourished in the 1920s and 1930s.

Set against these dehumanized characters marginally related to the film industry are other characters who are merely glimpsed and whom West calls "spectators." They are individuals from various parts of the country who have "come to California to die." They have no identity nor vitality, and no possibility exists in them for self-realization. Many of them, in retirement, have come to Los Angeles to be close to the dream-enrichment of the film capital, which seems all that sustains them in their starved lives. With a strange mixture of envy and bitterness, they stare "with hatred in their eyes" at the "players," the characters who have a semblance of "life" in their affiliation, however marginal, with Hollywood. With menacing glances, they wander through the

novel in search of transforming glamor. In a gruesome
sequence, two of their representatives appear at Harry
Greener's funeral, acting on an impression that he has an
association with films. It should be noted that a sexual
luridness is implied in West's description of them. One is
an old woman with "a face pulled out of shape by badly
fitting store teeth," which makes her mouth seem voracious; the other is an old man who, while seated in a back
chapel pew, "sucks on the handle of a home-made walking stick," an image suggesting an act of fellatio. They
have entered the funeral parlor in search of excitement,
afforded by their glimpsing a film-world death, and they
may be said to feed on death.

These people, the "spectators," appear en masse in the
novel's culminating scene before Kahn's Persian Palace
Theatre, by which a violet klieg light plays over the sky in
"wide crazy sweeps." In front of the theater an enormous
electric sign hangs over the middle of the street, announc-
ing: "MR. KAHN A PLEASURE DOME
DECREED," a parody of Coleridge's poem of a transcendent world above reality, to which the romantic
imagination has access. But the assumptions of Coleridge's "Kubla Khan" are mocked by the sterility implied
to exist in the film industry.[5] A radio announcer reports
the happenings of the premiere in a rapid hysterical voice
"like that of a revivalist preacher whipping his congrega-
tion toward an ecstasy of fits," but there can be no godly
revelation in the grotesque world West depicts, which is
mere vaudeville. The crowd before the "pleasure dome"
are all doomed in their illusion, are like passengers aboard
a ship bound for nowhere, are a "ship of fools."

Of the minor characters in The Day of the Locust, Abe
Kusich is a particularly brilliant conception. He could
easily have been a mere oddity, or a rather mechanical
symbol. But in fact he has been drawn with a deep impres-

sion of life—from the moment he first appears, after having been thrown out of a prostitute's room, until he drives off finally in his car, which has special extensions on the clutch and brake so that he can reach them with his tiny feet. Abe is captured distinctly in the special idioms of his speech, his half-finished sentences, and vernacular expressions, like "quiff" and "fingeroo." Virtually everything he says has the vividness of speech that has been closely listened to by West. In his idiosyncrasy but credibility, he is like a figure of fantasy who has been brought to life through the closest realism.

One of the most surprising features of the dwarf is his truculence, his way of compensating for his diminutive stature. West never attempts to explain Abe Kusich; he is merely presented in the oddity of his situation and personality. A chief oddity is his hyperactive sex drive, which has been undiminished by his standing only at the belt buckle of normally-sized men. Although his unwillingness to be defeated by his handicap is admirable, his sex life would not seem to be very rewarding. From what is known of him, it consists of transient encounters with prostitutes whom he despises and who despise him, and his life is wholly without love. His attraction to Faye Greener is pitiful not only because he cannot realistically hope to compete for her but also because, were he to have her, she would offer him nothing real.

Called "Honest Abe Kusich," he is a shrunken, unhappy parody of "Honest Abe Lincoln," the tall, presidential prophet of American democratic aspirations. "Honest Abe Kusich" is made to seem dubious in his aspirations, as a sexual combatant and as a racetrack tout; and his presence in the work implies that Lincoln's vision of brotherhood is deceptive too. (In one of the novel's moments of gruesomely comic parody, Homer Simpson is shown sorrowfully alone in his Hollywood cottage, and attempting to fill the emptiness and banality of his life sings the opening lines of the *Star-Spangled Banner*.) Abe's life consists of brutalization, and scarcely anything else. At the party in Homer's cottage, he viciously attacks Earle Schoop, squeezing his testicles until the cowboy collapses with pain. But Abe himself is then assaulted by Miguel, who seizes him by the ankles and "dashes him against the wall, like a man killing a rabbit against a tree." It is one of the fine things about West's treatment of Abe that, at least at one point, he makes his vulnerability touching. This moment occurs when Abe acts as the handler for "Big Red," the bird that is destroyed in a cockfight by a stronger adversary. Abe is shown stroking the game but inadequately equipped bird tenderly, and the reader understands that what exists between them is a kinship of the disabled in a remorselessly cruel world.

In a muted way, an element of vaudeville can be noted in West's treatment of Abe. When he first appears, entangled in the prostitute's bathrobe, he falls forward onto the floor, landing on his hands, like a figure in a slapstick routine. Later Tod comes to realize that his pugnacity is a joke among those who know him, and who play with him as if he were a growling puppy, "staving off his mad rushes and then baiting him to rush again." In effect, Abe becomes a comic performer in a world in which the idea of meaning is burlesqued. Absurdist vaudeville is implied at various points in the work, but it is expressed most strikingly in Harry Greener. Harry is enclosed so totally within a vaudeville identity that even when he is taken ill while peddling a spurious silver polish at Homer's cottage, he does not know how to react, other than in the form of clowning. His habitual clowning is closely related to his maiming since, as West notes, it is defensive; no one would be likely to "punish" a clown. Yet the clown is punished, after all, since his clowning keeps him from participating in "life." His laughter is ultimately, and always, at his own expense.

Harry's illusion is associated with the theater, the success he never had, the newspaper clipping he saves and carries with him that is meant to authenticate a past. The clipping, entitled "Bedraggled Harlequin," describes his performance with an aerial troupe called the Flying Lings. As the review explains, the Lings assault him from their trapezes, and in his attempts to evade them he does pratfalls onto the stage. The assaults continue and Harry becomes increasingly helpless, while the crowd roars with laughter. His performance is a prolonged humiliation, and it is a summary of his life, which West has sketched briefly. Harry had begun with the aspiration of becoming a Shakespearean actor, hardship followed, and his dreams went unrealized. During his descent to the commonest level of show business, he married a dancer who proved to be notoriously unfaithful, and eventually ran off with a magician. Out of work, he came to California with his daughter, hoping to find work in films doing slapstick routines, but was never employed. Little wonder that the strange laugh he practices is called "a victim's laugh."

Harry has, in fact, a large assortment of unsettling laughs that he works up. His favorite one, West notes, "began with a sharp, metallic crackle, like burning shrieks, then gradually increased in volume until it became a rapid bark, then fell back again to another obscene chuckle. After a slight pause, it climbed until it was a nicker of a horse, then still higher to become a machine-like screech." This insane laugh is a medley of degradations—of sounds like the inarticulate cries of dogs and horses; the chuckling of cheap, leering lust; and the mechanical screech of dehumanization. Like Harry's life, the medley of sounds is incoherent. A superb moment in the novel occurs when Harry is stricken at Homer's cottage, and appears in the doorway of the living room in the imagery of a clown. "His nose was very red," West writes, "but the rest of his face was drained white and he seemed to have grown too small for his clothing." Nor is he spared in his death, which has the mocking emptiness of a macabre jest. In his casket at the funeral parlor, his faced "touched up" with rouge by the undertaker, he is said to look like "the interlocutor in a minstrel show."

The funeral parlor itself, with its imitation stained-glass windows and fake oak-paneled walls, gives an eerie impression of soullessness. It is, in fact, very much like a theater, a theater for death. As the service is about to begin, the overhead lights dim, like the house lights of a theater, and accenting lights go on. There is in this scene no sense of a family gathered together in mourning. Harry's "family" consists only of Faye, who emits "artificial sobs, modulated according to appropriateness," and a few, unemployed film extras like the Gingos. The funeral parlor is nearly empty, and seems like a cheap, poorly attended theater. Other small details add to the sense of hollowness in the scene. The funeral, for example, has been arranged by a janitress at the San Berdoo, who is efficient in clearing away trash and debris. And the people who wander in from the street, thinking that Harry may be someone of importance in films, only to decide that he isn't and to leave, emphasize the wholly exiguous nature of his life and death.

Unlike Harry, who appears only in the early part of the novel, Faye is present throughout, and is a focal figure in the work. Hollywood actresses had been treated with harsh satire before *The Day of the Locust*, particularly in the fiction of John O'Hara and John Dos Passos. Dos Passos's Margo Dowling in *The Big Money* (1938), the final installment of his *U.S.A.* trilogy, is a scathing portrait of banality and vacancy. But Faye is not established in films at all, and in type has affinities with the "town tease," enclosed within her own narcissism, who appears in Faulkner's fiction. Sketched in acid, she is seen as Cec-

ily Saunders in *Soldiers' Pay* and as Temple Drake in
Sanctuary, the latter of which, in its passages of grotesque
comedy, can be compared with West's work.[6] But Faye is
not quite like any of these other women. West's conception of her is abstract, yet somehow plausible, so that she
is real and yet also an embodiment of American dreaming.

Faye is, in part, played off against her father who, in
Hollywood, has reached the final stage of his pitiful show
business career, while she is young and upwardly aspiring
in the entertainment industry. But it should be noted that
they are not wholly different. Harry is always acting, and
so is Faye. His acting, indeed, has come to deprive him of
any real self. West observes that he "had very little back
or top to his head. It was almost all face, like a mask, with
deep furrows between the eyes, across the forehead and
on either side of the nose and mouth, plowed there by
years of broad grinning and heavy frowning. Because of
them, he could never express anything either subtly or
exactly. They wouldn't permit degrees of feeling, only
the furthest degree." Faye is similarly over-projected and
without personal identity, so that there is literally
nothing about her that can be called real. She is so conscious of herself, even to her smallest gestures, that it is as
if she were aware of cameras upon her, or were practicing
for them. In an early scene at Homer's cottage, she turns
"at the waist without moving her legs, so that her snug
dress twisted even tighter," showing her dainty arched
ribs and petite waist. But she is not posing for anyone in
particular; her provocative movement is automatic, part
of a repertoire of gestures that may be produced at any
time. A few moments later, she breaks into her rendition
of "Jeepers Creepers," trucking, jerking her buttocks and
shaking her head from side to side. When this preposterous performance is concluded, she sits at a table eating
gingersnaps with a delicate crunching sound and drinking

coffee, holding the cup so that smallest finger "curls away from the rest of her hand." All these gestures, whether brassy or ladylike, are equally without meaning, since they are merely coy overtures to sex or forms of sexual enticement.

The vacancy of her mind is seen in the sequence in which she tells Tod of her idea for a film, which will be concerned with a girl at sea. When her wealthy father's yacht is wrecked in a storm, the beautiful but spoiled heroine is washed ashore on a tropical island. There, while bathing naked in a brook, she is seized by a huge snake, but is rescued opportunely by a handsome sailor who had been on the yacht and been rebuffed by her for his lack of social position. It now turns out that he, too, is rich, and been working as a sailor merely for adventure. Her idea is a parody of a thousand vapid films that are supposedly about love but are actually sexual fantasies. Faye tells Tod that she has "hundreds and hundreds" of other story ideas, but it is evident that they are all versions of the sexual dreaming that has produced her and that she embodies.

But Faye is not merely comic, although she is that. She has the "swordlike legs" of a castrater, and West, who really feels her power, evokes her at times in imagery of terror and death. Her invitation, he remarks, "wasn't to pleasure but to struggle, hard and sharp, closer to murder than to love. If you threw yourself on her, it would be like throwing yourself from the parapet of a skyscraper. You would do it with a scream. You couldn't expect to rise again. Your teeth would be driven into your skull like nails in a pine board and your back would be broken. You wouldn't even have time to sweat or close your eyes." The male sexual fear implied in this passage can be noticed elsewhere in the novel—even when West is mocking Faye or condescending to her. Violence and dehumanization seem to follow her wherever she goes, as can be seen in a series of superbly controlled scenes that begin with her visit to the mountain camp in the Hollywood hills.

The mountain-camp scene is set at the height of spring, but nature is presented ambivalently; it is bright and inviting, yet ominous, and suggests absolute heartlessness. The canyons give an eerie feeling of emptiness, and bright poppies along the path seem oddly artificial, their petals "wrinkled like crepe." In the sky overhead a blue jay is pursued swiftly by its natural enemy the hummingbird, and their darting movement of fierce pursuit and attempted evasion bursts the air apart into glittering particles "like metal confetti," an image that suggests the celebration of a wedding, but of some strangely inhuman kind.

The scene is orchestrated with a number of motifs–of dancers, song, and birds–that appear at other points in the work. A quail calls, and is answered by a quail in Miguel's trap, a sound that is full of hopelessness and melancholy. Before long Miguel takes some of the birds from the trap, and wrings their necks. His preparing the birds for their meal has been given sexual connotations, since the "eating" ritual is linked with the sexual one; and when they begin to eat, Miguel and Faye exchange sexual glances. Nor does one forget the cruel, ultimately sexual, intimations of Miguel's "plucking" of the birds–the way in which their feathers fall to the ground point first, "weighed down by the tiny drop of blood that trembled on the tips of their quills."

The entire scene has been created with a very close observation of detail, and with an intensity of mood reminiscent of D. H. Lawrence; and it builds suspensefully, and with a sense of inevitability, toward its climax. Earle and Miguel are figures drawn in mere outline; neither has any deeply personal identity. Miguel is remembered for his wiry black hair and his "black lips," and as a type he is purely physical. He is the "Mexican," who has no last name, and Earle is a "wooden, formal" cowboy who has no definition to his face and expresses himself in sudden outbursts of violence. They become drawn into a sexual ritual that centers upon Faye; it begins with Miguel's tearing the flesh and bone of the dead quail with a pair of heavy tin shears. Faye holds her hands over her ears so as not to have to hear the cruel click of the blades, but she is also aroused by the rending of flesh, and becomes increasingly excited as Miguel sings a song, and she drinks tequila.

The lyrics of his song ("The boys in Havana love Tony's wife") suggest sexual combat, and the dance that Miguel and Faye engage in has a similar implication. Essentially, it is a mating-hunting ritual belonging to nature before the time of civilization, and its overtones are "inhuman" and predatory. The dancers, Miguel and Faye, become abstract, like figures in a stylized ballet choreographed by a mindless natural world. They no longer possess individual will, and it is as if they are drugged by the ritual they enact. The scene ends in ir-rational violence, as Earle, excluded from the dance, assaults Miguel, and Faye flees. Her sudden disappearance at this point is similar in type to her later disappearances in the novel, after she has brought men to sexual arousal and excited violence.

The Day of the Locust is West's most cinematic novel,[7] and is intensely visual in effect. It moves in a sequence of episodes that are captured as a camera would record them, and has a supple ease of transition and adjustment of focus. But the episodes are all closely related, even if their interrelation is not immediately apparent. The mountain-camp scene, for instance, although so self-contained that it could be abstracted from the novel, has been linked with a later episode set at Homer's garage. The cockfight staged at the garage is attended not only by Tod but also by Claude Estee, and

Estee's presence there implies a connection between what happens and Hollywood itself.

The cockfight takes place, West remarks, during "one of those blue and lavender nights when the luminous color seems to have been blown over the scene with an air brush." Hollywood glamor, however, does not conceal the hard reality of night, which the cockfight represents. It is a skillfully managed scene that contains no direct authorial comment by West, and needs none. The birds are set loose in combat, which is closely and painstakingly described, and at the end one of them is "destroyed." Hermano (a name that in Spanish means "brotherhood") or "Big Red" has its beak torn off and its eye pierced by Juju's gaff; and even as "Big Red" lies dead Juju pecks obscenely at its remaining eye. The combat has been mindless, dictated by the nature of the cocks to compete for the female of the species. What is witnessed between them is, as West had said of Faye's invitation to pleasure, "closer to murder than to love."

The scene of the cockfight, in turn, prepares for the party at Homer's cottage, when Faye "peacocks" for the men. To Claude Estee, Faye babbles about wanting to get a start in films, a subject that elicits her full repertoire of gestures. She wets her lips, smiles, laughs, shivers, crosses and uncrosses her legs, widens and narrows her eyes, tosses her platinum hair so that it "splashes" against the red plush of a chair back. Her gestures are an anthology of countless films that, although vacant, exert a sexual fascination. The song Faye sings at the party, "I'm a vi-pah," is a call to opiation, since a viper, in the argot of the thirties, was a drug user; and as a "wail" and "dirge," it is associated with death.

Before long the song leads to a "mating dance," similar to the one at the mountain camp, between Faye and several of the men; and this in turn is followed by an outburst of violence prompted by Abe, who has been excluded. It should be noted that in the course of the scene Faye is progressively *stripped*. At the opening of the scene she wears a pair of green silk lounging pajamas, but as the men compete for her the garment becomes torn. A sleeve is ripped off, and the trousers are shredded. At the height of the melee, she steps out of the trousers, so that she is wearing only her "tight black lace drawers," and announces that she is going to bed. In the bedroom she is at last naked, and it is here, while she is mounted by Miguel, that Earle appears and another scene of ferocious violence takes place. The scene ends in confusion, with Faye screaming, and pulling a sheet over her face. It is one of the brilliant strokes of the novel that, in this final stripping of her, Faye should horrify even herself.

The novel is told from Tod's point of view, and he is present in almost all of the scenes. Through him, West is able to move back and forth between the dispossessed Angelenos and the film studios, and to call particular attention to the costuming, props, and unreal sets of the sound stages. At one point, for example, he notices a group of men and women in riding costumes who are picnicking on a "lawn of fiber," and eat "cardboard food" in front of a "cellophane waterfall." They suggest a whole world of sham and devitalization, just as another set that Tod comes upon, a Greek temple dedicated to Eros before which the god lies "face downward in a pile of old newspapers and bottles," announces the theme of the death of love.

After Faye leaves the San Berdoo, Tod catches sight of her on the studio lots, and goes searching for her. He is unable to find her, because she is as unreal as the sets themselves. The sets, which include half a Mississippi riverboat and a Western building with a façade but no interior, are encountered by him without pattern or coherent order, so that they seem like flotsam and jetsam—the final "dream dump" of American culture. In *Balso Snell* and "The Adventurer," West speaks of grotesques who spend their days in libraries poring over books, to find only a nightmare of fragmentary images from the past. But in *The Day of the Locust*, fragmentation and loss of identity are imagined through the meaningless sets. Tod's search for Faye reaches its climax when he finds himself on the set of *Waterloo*, where the charge up the slope of Mont St. Jean becomes a debacle. The still unfinished set caves in, swallowing "Napoleon's army with painted cloth." The collapse of the *Waterloo* set repeats the catastrophe suffered by Napoleon, but the Hollywood version is mere slapstick, a vaudeville of dehumanization.

An important function Tod serves in the novel is to foreshadow events to come, sometimes in the form of delicately constructed symbolic scenes in which he appears. An example is the scene at Audrey Jennings's call house, where Tod, with Claude Estee and his guests, go to see a prurient film. The film, *Le Predicament de Marie*, opens with a tantalizing situation, promising titillation for every sexual appetite. When the film breaks at a particularly enticing point, the guests stage a mock riot, stamping their feet and shouting "fake, cheat." The episode, handled with restrained understatement by West, looks ahead to the crowd scene at the end, where those who have been "cheated" and deceived by Hollywood go on a rampage.

More particularly, Tod's foreshadowing role grows out of his peculiar situation as a culturally uprooted man, and artist or "seer." He has been hired by Hollywood after finishing his undergraduate work at the Yale School of Fine Arts, and placed where he is, it is inevitable that he should pursue Faye, who is Hollywood in essence. Tod is said to be a New Englander by "race, training, and heritage," but in Hollywood he is singularly powerless—so much so that he comes increasingly to assume the role of a prophet of doom. His fruitless pursuit of Faye is a long frustration, and it is accompanied, even at the opening, by his imagining of destruction. His painting, "The Burning of Los Angeles," which has affinities with the paintings of James Ensor,[8] but was probably inspired by West's own early poem "Burn the Cities,"[9] is already being planned by him when the novel opens. His preliminary sketches, in the manner of Goya's and Daumier's mocking caricatures, are to contain scenes of hollow-eyed, forsaken ones who have come to Hollywood to die.

Tod's conception of the painting evolves with each of his encounters with Faye. After she tells him of her idea for a film that is a vulgar sexual daydream and tease, he is filled with a desire to rape her, "to throw her down in the soft, warm mud and to keep her there." And in his mind he imagines new drawings that he will do for the painting. They will show a naked girl being chased by a mob. She has a strange, rather mocking expression of sexual release on her face, and a woman in pursuit is about to throw a rock at her to bring her down. This new conception brings the "cheated" ones into focus by putting them in relation to Faye in a scene of revenge that is like Tod's own sex-and-murder fantasy.

At the end of the mountain-camp scene, Tod actually chases Faye through the hills with the intention of raping her. He stumbles and falls, is out of breath, and cannot find her; can only dream his revenge in the form of his painting-to-be. In this latest conception, the city of Los Angeles will be on fire, but there will be a gala air to the scene; a holiday crowd will burn the city. The gala crowd at the premiere is now forecast, and the painting is all but complete. It needs only one finishing touch, supplied when Tod pursues Faye through the fantastic labyrinth of studio sets. With Faye's eluding him once again, he envisions the painting in the tortured, baroque style of Salvator Rosa and the other painters of Decay and Mystery.

He sees it now in terms of all the cruelty and barbarism that exist in life.

With the scene of the premiere, Tod's painting becomes "realized"; it is painted in his mind in the same sequence in which the mayhem takes place before the theater. In this vision of holocaust, the city is in flames, its incoherently designed houses are all burning. In the middle foreground a mob of cheated ones, who had expected fulfillment in their lives from Hollywood, surge forward carrying baseball bats and torches, intent on purifying the world with destruction. Formerly "spectators," they become "performers," or participants. Fleeing from the "crusading mob" are Faye, Harry (clutching his vaudevillian's derby hat), and Homer, "falling out of the canvas . . . his big hands clawing the air in anguished pantomime." The crowd's wrath is indiscriminate, claiming Homer as well as the Greeners; and this sense of a confused fury in the painting merges with what occurs literally before the theater, so that the reader is forced to respond to the crowd scene *as if* it were part of Tod's painting.

The crowd scene gives the novel its climax, but it leads nowhere, since the people who make up the crowd lack identity and in the mayhem find none. They merely release their own anarchic impulses, of which sexuality is significantly a part. A young girl's silk dress is torn down the front, and her brassiere hangs from one strap, while an old man wearing a Panama hat and horn-rimmed glasses has one hand inside her dress and is biting her neck. This startling image is a refocusing of an earlier one in which Faye's silk lounging pajamas are torn at the party by the men who struggle to get at her; and their likeness intimates the crowd's frustration is an enlarged version of the frustration and destructiveness implied in Faye and the Hollywood illusion industry.

The final scene suggests a theme that *The Day of the Locust* has in common with *Miss Lonelyhearts*, inasmuch as both novels deal with the entrapment of people within media illusion. The marginal people in *Miss Lonelyhearts* write to "Miss L" for deliverance from their misery, and in *The Day of the Locust* wretched people look to Hollywood. Yet nothing can save these people, or even the protagonists of these novels. In *Miss Lonelyhearts*, Betty and Pete Doyle converge on "Miss L" as he stands at the stairway landing, blocking his escape. If Betty represents an unthinking acceptance of the "given," Pete implies rebellion that is incoherent and destructive. Caught between the two, "Miss L" can achieve no identity and must die. Something like this happens to Tod in *The Day of the Locust*. His immersion in Hollywood illusion permits him no identity, but there is no escape for him, for at the end he confronts the frenzied disorder of the crowd, rebellion that is merely chaos.

If Tod does not actually die at the end, his continued existence can at least no longer be imagined, and is in effect extinguished. Fittingly, Tod's name in German means "death," and it is worth noting that the mob scene is set in motion by a death—that of Adore. The rumor that a pervert has attacked a child excites an unnatural craving for excitement in the people who have come to the premiere, and are themselves the living dead. Only the most lurid excitement can bring them to a semblance of life. The impression that the scene gives is one of absolute dehumanization, and Tod's final gesture, his imitating the "wail" of the police car siren, signals if not his actual death then at least his psychic withdrawal from the world.

In closing out the world, Tod, as it were, returns to the womb—an idea anticipated in West's conception of other characters. Abe Kusich, for instance, is first seen sleeping blissfully in the bundle of the prostitute's bathrobe, which swallows him within its folds and suggests a womb. The idea is insinuated later when Faye retreats into the darkness under the sheet that she pulls over her face. But it is presented most memorably in West's depiction of Homer, who in his dreams crawls down a tunnel toward a patch of darkness at the end. After the savagery of the party, he goes into a catatonic state, recoiling into a fixed position with his knees drawn up to his chin, so that he resembles a fetus. Like Homer, who is appalled by the horror of life, Tod withdraws at the end into a preconscious state.

Randall Reid has argued that Homer Simpson evolves from Sherwood Anderson's gallery of "grotesques" in *Winesburg, Ohio*,[10] and that he has strong affinities in particular with Wing Biddlebaum, the schoolteacher whose flighty hands betray his anxiety and radical helplessness. In a daring move, Reid maintains, West brings Anderson's troubled and inarticulate Midwesterner to the West Coast, where he finds not release from his inner trouble but degradation and disillusionment. There is certainly a resemblance, at least, between the two characters, but it should be remembered that Homer is less realistic a conception than Wing Biddlebaum. If Wing Biddlebaum is maimed, he is nevertheless recognizably "human," and sympathetic, whereas Homer's lack of identity is so radical that he can hardly be called "human" at all. He is like a bundle of incoherent gestures, and in many ways he is so infantile that he seems to struggle merely to be "born" into life. In this respect, he is a figure who embodies the inchoate longings of middle America.

In Wayneville, Iowa, Homer seems like a man only half awake. The critical incident of his life as a hotel bookkeeper in his encounter with Romola Martin, an unhappy alcoholic tenant whom the manager sends Homer to evict. In her bedroom, he is aroused by her sympathetically and erotically, and he gives her all the money in his wallet. He touches her fumblingly, and she laughs at him—while taking the money and departing from the scene. Soon after, while recovering from a "cold," which seems psychosomatic, he quits his job and moves to Hollywood to take an early retirement. In Hollywood, he is a little closer to something; he is not sure what it is, but surely it is related to his arousal by Romola Martin. In his pathetic cottage he sits listlessly, imagining that a breeze outside his window makes a sound like that of "silk stirring against silk." He sobs and waits. Before long Faye Greener appears at his door.

Homer qualifies as a "grotesque" by his unruly hands, which have a life of their own. He is unable to control their writhing movements, and in an early, and eerie, scene they "sleep" even after he has awakened. He is said to "carry" his hands into the bathroom where he places them in a basin of cold water. "They lay quietly on the bottom," West observes, "like a pair of strange aquatic animals. When they were thoroughly chilled and began to crawl about, he lifted them out and hid them in a towel." The water imagery perfectly captures the sense of his hands as his subconscious. The strange aquatic animals at the bottom of the water (like an ocean floor) represent his latent sexuality, which his conscious mind censors or disavows. In the scene in which he meets Faye, his fingers "twined like a tangle of thighs in miniature," and he has to sit on them to keep them quiet. In the late episode in which Faye dances in his cottage, he goes outside to sit on the curb, and here his fingers involuntarily play "here's the church and here's the steeple," a "manual ballet" that evokes his desire to join in the dance. More particularly, the steeple-making movements of his fingers show him struggling toward a state of erection.

In an ironic way, Homer has been given a Christlike implication by West. He has Christlike attributes of "resignation, kindliness, and humility," and he is sexually abstinent. Gentle and unworldly, he undergoes a martyrdom in the course of the work. His role as a mock version of Christ is implied in the scene of Harry Greener's funeral, which has strongly sexual overtones. In order to pay for the funeral, Faye goes to work for Audrey Jennings as a call girl. She finds the expedient distasteful, since it does not conform to her image of herself as a future film star; is unwilling to discuss the incident with Tod, and would like to deny that it has occurred. But it is the realest thing about her—that is, that she is a whore. Even while Harry lies in his casket, Tod, in the corridor beyond the chapel, entreats Faye to have sex with him, pawing her and nearly tearing her dress, an incident that adds a sense of desecration to the funeral scene.

During the same scene, as the funeral service begins, an electric organ plays a recording of a Bach chorale, "Come Redeemer, Our Saviour," entreating Christ to appear. One thing that is peculiar about the recording, however, is that it is subtly mocking. Christ is invited to appear in a casual manner that suggests "you may if you wish," as a woman might invite the attention of a man—not too eagerly but with subdued signals of interest. The Bach chorale, in effect, becomes a sexual tease. In the following sequence, Faye moves into the cottage with Homer, the mock Christ. Their sharing the cottage is a version of their living together as lovers, but there is, of course, no sex—only a constant, although hopeless, reminder to Homer of Faye's sexuality. Faye explains to Tod that the arrangement is on a very proper, businesslike basis. Homer provides food and lodging and buys the dresses Faye needs, and she will reimburse him with interest when she becomes a star. She even wants to have the arrangement certified formally by a lawyer. But Faye is merely exploiting Homer, taking advantage of his naive nature. Moreover, his proximity to her is no blessing. The dresses he pays for are a symbolic version of her body, which he cannot have but of which he must be ever

conscious, if only in the form of his unruly hands. At the
scene of the party, Homer is so unhappy that he goes outside to sit on the curb beside Tod, where his fingers struggle to make "steeples," until Tod tells him to stop "for
Christ's sake."

The destructiveness implied in Faye is seen in her
relationship to the men who compete for her, but it is also
kept before the reader by her special relationship to
Homer. In earlier works, West had played with the idea
of the "dog" as an anagram of "God," a mocking version
of man's condition; and this idea is introduced again in
The Day of the Locust. Abe Kusich and Harry Greener
are both presented at times in canine imagery, and so, in
his isolation and helplessness, is Homer. When he moves
into his cottage, for instance, he sobs pitifully in his
bathtub, making a sound "like that of a dog lapping
gruel." Later, when Homer shares the cottage with Faye,
Faye becomes bored and then irritated by his lack of
assertiveness. His servility, West comments, "was like
that of a cringing, clumsy dog, who is always anticipating
a blow, welcoming it even, and in a way that makes overwhelming the desire to strike him." At this point, irked
by his sexual failure, Faye has begun to "persecute"
Homer, and West observes that Homer is "destroying
himself."

While they still live together, Faye and Tod, with
Homer, go to the Cinderella bar, where a female impersonator performs. He sings in a soft, throbbing voice, and
as he croons he rocks an imaginary cradle with caressing
gestures. In effect, he becomes a woman. Just before he
performs, Faye remarks that she can't stand fairies, and in
a comically pathetic moment she asks Homer if he knows
what a fairy is. Tod attempts to help him by making the
word "homo" with his lips, but Homer, without understanding, says "Momo," and Faye remarks derisively,
"What a hick." In fact, the whole scene reveals Faye's

malicious humiliation of Homer. She forces brandy down his throat, so that some of it spurts out of his nose and soils his clothing; and when he is tight and attempts to enter into the spirit of the nightclub, he becomes an awkward "clown." He is degraded and debased by her, as other men are in scenes of violence.

One feature of the scene that should be noticed particularly is its implied contrast between Faye and the female impersonator. The contrast is handled skillfully, its effect kept deliberately muted, but it is telling. As Homer is humiliated with alcohol by Faye, the female impersonator croons a lullaby to a baby boy who is crying because someone has taken his kiddie car away, and must now be tucked in so that, in sleep, he can recover from the traumatic experience. Clearly the "little man" of the lullaby is Homer; and it is deeply ironic that the female impersonator can be maternal and tender while Faye, an actual woman, cannot.

In the early section of the novel, Faye and Harry Greener appear as character doubles, since both are enclosed within show-business illusion and cannot be authentic. But Faye has also been doubled with another character in the work, the child actor Adore Loomis. Just as Faye has been prepared for a film career by her father, Adore has been groomed for such a career by his mother. Maybelle Loomis, like Harry Greener, has a rich background in illusion—in her case, in the spuriousness of ersatz religion. In the section of the novel in which she appears, West refers to the new religions that flourish in California; and he even has Tod visit some of their churches—the "Church of Christ, Physical," which worships physical fitness; the "Temple Moderne," which imitates the breathing exercises of the Aztec tribes; and the "Tabernacle of the Third Coming," whose scripture is "a crazy jumble of dietary rules, economics and Biblical threats." Maybelle Loomis's guru is Dr. Pierce, the raw-food faddist, and while technically he is not at the head of a religion, he is by implication equivalent to being a religious leader. Billboard posters announce him as "Know-All Pierce-All," which gives him the Godlike attribute of omniscience. The name of Mrs. Loomis's child, Adore, implies that he is a kind of religious offering to her gods, the chief of which is the Hollywood film industry. She is as closely bound to show-business illusion as Harry Greener.

Faye and Adore are linked in their first appearances. Faye, who is seventeen, is "dressed like a child of twelve," in a white cotton dress with a blue sailor collar; and Adore, who is eight, is "dressed like a man," in long trousers, vest, and jacket. They are evoked as children of Hollywood, whose innocence has been warped. Adore is even called "the Frankenstein monster." He is innocence adulterated by the commodity values of the world, which have sexuality at their source. West has this in mind when he has Adore sing a song, "Mama Doan Wan No Peas," which he accompanies with sexually suggestive, buttocks-swinging movements. The song is a counterpart of Faye's "viper" song, which reveals her as a purveyor of a sexual narcotic. Faye and Adore are alike, moreover, in their being tormentors of Homer. Adore makes faces at him, while Faye mocks his sexual repression.

After the horror of the party, in which Homer comes face to face with the "inhumanness" implied in the character of Faye, and after she leaves him, Homer is reduced to inconsolable sobbing. Earlier he had been shown sobbing, and his sobbing was implied in the female impersonator's lullaby, but in the final cottage scene his sobbing become terrible. "He cried," West writes, "without covering his face or bending his head. The sound was like an ax chopping pine, a heavy, hollow, chunking noise. It was repeated rhythmically but without accent. There was no progress in it. Each chunk was exactly like the one that preceded. *It would never reach a climax"* (emphasis mine). The scene is all the more terrible because it implies that Homer is impotent. His torment is that of a man between two worlds. He cannot enter into the sexual life, but on the other hand, after his exposure to Faye, he can no longer close sexuality out of his mind. His suffering is thus raised to an unbearable level.

In his final appearance, Homer is seen dazed on the outskirts of the crowd at the premiere; he is untidily dressed and carries a suitcase in each hand, as he prepares to leave the city. His trousers have been pulled on over his cotton nightgown, and a piece of the garment hangs out of his open fly with the mocking effect of a "flannel penis." As he pauses to rest on a bench, Adore appears, and throws an opened purse, held by a string, by Homer's feet. He hopes that Homer will notice it and stoop to pick it up, imagining that he has made a valuable find—at which point Adore will snatch it away. But Adore's baiting of Homer with the opened purse is a sexual taunt, since the purse can be understood as a vaginal symbol. When Homer fails to respond, Adore throws a stone that strikes Homer in the face, and at this point, driven to distraction, Homer turns on his tormentor— Adore literally, but in a sense Faye. In stomping Adore underfoot, Homer is actually assaulting Faye; the stomping can even be seen as a symbolic form of rape.

That the stomping is sexual, and implies rape, is suggested in the frenzy it incites in the crowd of "excluded" ones. The scene of mayhem that ensues has the overtones of an orgy, which ends in pointless destruction. In earlier scenes, the sexual arousal of Abe Kusich and Earle Schoop, when they were excluded from the "dance," had led to incidents of wild violence; and the scene before the movie theater reenacts such violence on a vaster scale. It is imagined by West in an apocalyptic vision of Middle America, in its misery of exclusion, run amok, attempting vainly to find transcendence through a fevered sexuality.

The members of the crowd are all victims of their own deception, but *their* particular victim is Homer. Homer's desperate violence reveals how he has at last been destroyed by Faye, dehumanized by her; and he in turn is destroyed by the mob. In a passage in which there is both poetry and horror, Homer rises for a moment above the mass, is "shoved against the sky," his "jaw hanging as though he wanted to scream but couldn't." A hand then reaches up and catches him "by his open mouth and pulled him forward and down" under the churning feet of the mob. All the images of this passage are important: the sky, Homer's naive illusion of innocence; the hand, the repressed violence in Homer; the feet, the lowest extremity of man's body, sexuality itself. The scene is West's climactic staging of sex and murder.

The Day of the Locust and Fitzgerald's *The Last Tycoon* may be compared in some respects. They were written at approximately the same time, and were the last books West and Fitzgerald wrote before their early deaths in 1940. Both are about Hollywood, use Hollywood sets to create a sense of illusion, and deal with a central character's estrangement in the film capital. West had never seen *The Last Tycoon*, however, and it could not have affected his novel. But another of Fitzgerald's novels, *The Great Gatsby*, does appear to have been influential.[11] West's conception of Faye Greener, for example, seems indebted, partly, to Fitzgerald's of Daisy Fay. Their names are similar, and so are their natures. They are both teases, who seem to promise much, but offer only death and destruction. Daisy Fay is mannered and artificial, and Faye Greener is mannered emptiness itself. When West writes that Faye's secret smile "seemed to promise all sorts of undefined intimacies," he even appears to be calling the reader's attention to Daisy Fay as Faye's prototype. Her last name, Greener, is an echo, too, of the green light of hope motif in Fitzgerald's novel, and it is significant that when Faye entices the men at the party she wears lounging pajamas of green silk.

These female characters who offer treacherous romance to men are treated scathingly by Fitzgerald and West. The reader is swayed to regard Daisy Fay with the deepest scorn, and West spares Faye nothing in exposing her valuelessness. In a searing passage near the end, West imagines Faye as a pretty cork, gilt with a glittering fragment of a mirror set in its top, that bobs on the sea and is set down on a strange shore "where a savage with pork-sausage fingers and a pimpled butt picked it up and hugged it to his sagging belly. Tod recognized the fortunate man; he was one of Mrs. Jennings's customers."

Fitzgerald is suggested in the novel at times in the turn of West's wit, and in his use of miniaturized effects and delicately constructed symbolic scenes. But the certainty of Fitzgerald's influence is seen in his use of the Carraway figure in Tod Hackett. Tod and Homer are doubled, just as Carraway and Gatsby are; they are point-of-view characters whose conflicts are related to those of the characters they observe. Tod is reminiscent of Carraway as a figure a little off to the side of the main action, a privileged witness; and there is even a scene in the novel when Tod comes to resemble Carraway rather closely. Near the end of *The Day of the Locust*, West introduces an episode that is at least structurally similar to one in *The Great Gatsby*. Tod leaves the party with Claude Estee after the violent scene, but when he returns to the cottage the following day he learns from Homer what had happened later, which has been related not by Tod directly but from his point of view. In Fitzgerald's novel, Carraway visits Gatsby for the last time, and relates what Gatsby has now told him about his life. The scene captures the breakup of Gatsby's illusion, and at the same time it shows Carraway in a kind of guardian role to him. When Tod visits Homer at the cottage, he, too, has a concerned interest in the odd figure he has come to know, and who is now reduced to grieving in his incoherent house. In the following scenes, Gatsby and Homer are both killed, and the works end with a sense of nightmare.

But the similarity between Tod and Carraway ends at a certain point. Gatsby and Homer are the "observed" figures of their respective novels, but if Gatsby is a heroic figure, Homer is the reverse. Homer is a broken automaton even before he leaves Wayneville, Iowa; and the reader is barred from an identification with him because of his infantility and incoherence. Gatsby and Homer are both victims, but while some meaning is implied in Gatsby's romantic imagination, none is suggested in Homer's incoherence. Homer's death does not ennoble him, but reveals the violence and sexuality within him that he has repressed, and that in turn are present in the other characters, who belong to a mere vaudeville of vacancy. The meanness of West's vision is a kind of scaling down of Fitzgerald's to the level of absolute empty brutality.

Ironically, just as Fitzgerald had difficulty bringing Carraway into a sharp personal focus, West has difficulties with Tod. He is the weakest of the major characters in *The Day of the Locust*, and, to be frank, he fails to come to life. There is too much about him that is merely putative—his New England and Yale Art School background, for instance, which are thinly and unconvincingly specified. Although Tod seems to know his art history, it is hard to imagine him doing any work as a set designer at the Hollywood studio. He is said, at the beginning, to be a very complicated young man "with a whole set of personalities, one inside the other like a nest of Chinese boxes," but his complicated nature is never demonstrated or even suggested.

Tod was apparently intended to be a version of Dostoyevsky's dual characters, like West's own Miss Lonelyhearts; but his conflict tends to seem fabricated. Partly because of his intelligence and detachment, it is difficult to picture him tearing at Faye's clothes or bent upon raping her as he pursues her through the wooded terrain beyond the mountain camp. The problem is that while his hatred of Faye is real enough, he knows her too well to be taken in by her. What is most credible about Tod is his hysteria, but this, too, is puzzling, since its nature is unclear. In the course of the work he harbors ever more ferocious visions of destruction, but they seem to be compelled by something other than Hollywood's bad taste or Faye's inaccessibility. James F. Light has remarked that Tod's "insistence upon falsity everywhere eventually seems a little overdone," and certainly one feels that Tod's vision of murderous violence as the virtual equivalent of sexuality is at times hysteric.

West also seems in trouble with his ending. The riot at the premiere has been memorably imagined, and been prepared for elaborately in the course of the work. Yet, despite all this, it seems somehow forced. The Angelenos begin to riot, one feels, too much on cue. One problem is that they are vague, sullen figures who exist on the fringes of the novel, and have never been brought very strongly to life. Although it is possible to imagine their disillusionment with Hollywood as a fulfilling experience, it is more difficult to picture them erupting into apocalyptic fury.

West's portrayal of Tod also raises questions about his sexuality, and makes one wonder if he is all that he seems to be. He clearly has a problem. His sexual passivity, accompanied by his mounting anger, suggests it. He is the passive-hysteric type who appears in various guises in West's earlier fiction—in Balso Snell, for example, and in Miss Lonelyhearts. Tod does not qualify as someone Faye might become interested in because he does not make enough money and is not handsome. But his chief

disqualification is his lack of force. In one scene Earle
Schoop rivets Faye with a deep kiss that suggests an even
more intimate sexual act, and Tod merely stands by, as if
he felt unequal to what he witnesses. When he pursues
Faye, bent on rape, he stumbles and falls rather easily, is
too short of breath to rise, and is thus spared the imagined
encounter with her. With each failure of his virility, he
dreams his revenge in the form of a modern holocaust, a
weakling's imagined retaliation upon the world.

That Tod is doubled with Homer there can be no
doubt. Tod's "large, sprawling body," West writes at the
beginning, "his slow blue eyes and sloppy grin made him
seem . . . almost doltish." This description cannot be
taken seriously, since it conflicts with the sense one has of
Tod's essential urbanity, and it seems included solely to
reinforce his kinship with Homer, to draw attention to
their affinity. Homer's sexuality is dormant and can
hardly express itself. He is like a child, able to feel Faye's
attraction, but unable to act on it–as if doing so were
under a grave taboo. Indeed, what is striking about
Homer's sexuality is its ambiguousness. His first
temptress is Romola Martin, who wears a "man's black
silk dressing gown," and has "close-cropped hair" that
makes her look like "a little boy." What West seems to be
suggesting is that Romola Martin allures Homer with a
kind of innocent, preadult sexuality; the brutal reality of
her sexuality, implied in her drunkenness and escapism,
he does not quite understand. But that she should attract
him as a "boy" is most peculiar.

At the Cinderella nightclub, as has been mentioned,
Faye asks Homer if he knows what a "fairy" is, and he is
confused by the term. Really, he does not seem to know
very much about the sexual life at all. At the scene of the
party, he lurks in a corridor off the living room, peeking
at Faye and the men who dance with her, and he claims,
innocently enough, to be happy that they are having a

good time. Later when he is in bed, naked, he hears Faye moan and, imagining that she must be in pain, goes to her room to find her being straddled by Miguel. A violent scene quickly follows, and Homer is reduced to trauma by his discovery of what sexuality means. As he now comes to learn, it means horror. Homer's peeking, however, implies that he is not as innocent as he would like to think. His lying naked in bed while Faye lies naked in the adjoining bedroom, an exact duplicate of his, implies that Homer's deepest horror is his discovery of the sexuality in himself. But is the unbearable guilt he feels due to his desire for Faye or to his identification with her, as the sexual partner of the Mexican?

When Faye sings her "viper" song at the party, Homer leaves to join Tod, seated on the curb before the house, who also has a "problem" with women. Homer is concerned about Faye's drinking, and the disturbing presence of Miguel and Earle in his garage, and he seeks advice from Tod. He calls him "Toddie," and with "trembling signals of affection," slips his hand into Tod's. At this moment they resemble Miss Lonelyhearts and Pete Doyle in their hand-holding; and there seems a homosexual dimension to the character of Homer at this point. Sexual ambiguousness appears again in the final scene when Homer stomps upon Adore. In doing so, he destroys himself, since Adore is a child, like himself in effect, and Adore's innocence is actually corrupt. The stomping can be read as a sexual assault upon Faye, who embodies the conflict in Homer between his innocence and his sexuality. Yet *literally* the object of his frustration and sexually related assault is a boy. The scene may be interpreted in different ways.

If Homer at last explodes into violence because of his sexual guilt, what would this say about his double, Tod? Tod shares with Homer a quality of helplessness—a very deep helplessness, in fact. Homer discovers that sexuality is malignant only at the end, while Tod has known it all along, and is still a victim of what he knows. He cannot reconcile his physical desires with his knowledge that a woman's body is, as Odo of Cluny had said, a sac of filth, treacherously corrupt. Homer's writhing hands are said to express his pain, and beneath his pleasing manners Tod is consumed with pain. His cherished vision of mayhem and destruction is an expression of it, and the apocalyptic ending is nothing if not a staging of his own gigantic sexual frustration—epic punishment visited upon himself and others who are tainted by sexuality.

Homer does not know what a "fairy" is, but Tod does. The impression of a latent homosexuality in Tod cannot be traced to anything very specific that happens in the novel. His masochism is obvious, since it is at the heart of his relationship to Faye. There is a voyeuristic streak in him too, since he is the recurring spectator of the sexuality of men more virile than himself. Otherwise, it is hard to pin him down, for, like Carraway, he gives the sense of having many secrets, which are kept out of view. One feature of his inner life is intriguing however—his paranoia.

A paranoiac vision of victimization exists in all of West's novels. It can be seen in *Balso Snell*, in which the protagonist is the victim of life, of women, and, finally, of his own body. It is apparent in *Miss Lonelyhearts*, in which the hero is the martyr of the world and of his complexes; and it is abundantly evident in *A Cool Million*, in which Lemuel Pitkin is the dupe of a treacherous father figure, and is endlessly maimed before he is at last killed. In *The Day of the Locust* the sense of victimization is magnified by the fact that virtually all the characters, including the most marginal onlookers, are victims. Homer is an exemplary victim, and Tod is a victim who harbors a meditated vision of revenge. His revenge is embodied in his painting, which yearningly anticipates the doom and destruction of Hollywood, of a whole world that has conspired to oppress him and to misuse his talents. The novel is filled with a sense of treachery, not only Hollywood's but even more pervasively and threateningly that of sexuality; and what is particularly relevant here is the Freudian corrolation between the paranoid personality and latent homosexuality—which can be surmised in Tod, and in West himself.

An odd feature of *The Day of the Locust* is that although it is seriously flawed it has often been brilliantly imagined. Novels with a Hollywood setting or theme had appeared before *The Day of the Locust*,[12] but compared to West's work they are extremely crude. Many novels about Hollywood have been written since,[13] but none of these reveals as piercing an imagination or leaves such a strong effect on the reader's mind. Harry Greener, Faye, Abe, and Homer are all great conceptions, real and at the same time vaudeville figures in an empty world. *The Day of the Locust* is more realistic than *Miss Lonelyhearts* in the social definition it gives to a particular environment. But in another sense it is romantic, metaphysical even in the conflict that exists between aspiration and a mysterious thwarting or stunting that is at the very basis of life and is all-powerful.

A parable of evil, *The Day of the Locust* is comic and horrible at once, and sometimes actually repelling, but it has an unusual quality of rareness, so that it is as if nothing exactly like the novel had ever existed in the past or could again. The novel began with a ship-of-fools conception, and in its completed form that conception can still be made out. The work is like a poetic conceit, in which a gallery of fools are mocked in their failed transcendence by their own animality. West's characters, some of whom are grotesque but all of whom have stunted lives and natures, have been styled as players in an absurd comedy; and in this dimension particularly his career in fiction concludes as it began—with the drama of human absurdism. It is this that is the sum of West's career.

6

Conclusion

In his essay, "West's Disease,"[1] W. H. Auden remarked that West "is not, strictly speaking, a novelist; that is to say, he does not attempt an accurate description either of the social scene or of the subjective life of the mind." Neither the incidents nor the language of *Balso Snell* seem to him credible as a transcription of a real dream; and the later novels, although set in recognizable places, violate the most rudimentary canons of plausibility. Auden argues that it is impossible to believe in Miss Lonelyhearts as an advice-columnist, since such columns are written by men of an entirely more practical turn of mind, and were there really such editors as Shrike, who are devoted to exposing to their employees the meaninglessness of journalism, they would not last long on their jobs. Nowhere in West's novels, moreover, are there any recognizably normal relationships: "No married couples have children, no child has more than one parent, a high percentage of the inhabitants are cripples, and the only kind of personal relation is the sadomasochistic." All the novels end in an escape from the conscious ego, and what lies behind this, Auden maintains, is "a hatred of oneself and every being one holds responsible for oneself."

A sufferer from "West's disease," Auden argues, is not selfish but "absolutely self-centered." Other people exist for him only as projections of his inner states; his pity toward them and his hatred of them are equally transferences of his attitudes toward himself. Ultimately the sufferer from "West's disease" craves physical pain. "As used by West," Auden concludes, "the cripple is, I believe, a symbolic projection of the state of wishful self-despair, the state of those who will not accept themselves in order to change themselves into what they would or should become, and justify this refusal by thinking that being what they are is uniquely horrible and uncurable."

In some respects Auden is right about West. Sadomasochism and self-condemnation are at the center of his work. Suffering is a chief tenet of his vision, and no cure for it is posited as being possible. But when Auden denies that West is a satirist, on the grounds that he is wholly lacking in detachment from that which he satirizes, he takes from West his very genuine claim to attention. West was one of the notable satirists of his period, but his work defies many of the conventional elements of plausibility and does not belong wholly to realistic fiction. His vision is absolutist, offering no alternative framework of values by which aberration can be measured. It has, one might say, an aesthetic autonomy, is a self-contained world in which the reader is forced to share the "absurd" suffering of West's characters.

Essentially West's comedy is that of nonexistence, since his characters only play at having authentic lives. In many cases, these characters are like cartoons, individuals who have only comic-strip identities. Fay Doyle beats her crippled husband with a newspaper, and the reader laughs, but partly at the way in which they have been placed within a cartoon frame, so that they cannot evolve into the fully human. The cripple is not merely, as Auden asserts, a symbol of "wishful self-despair." He is an Everyman figure confronted by the reality of his unimportance, by his failure to find any meaningful pattern in his life. He is a satiric magnification of a general existential situation.

West's drama of nonexistence begins with *Balso Snell*, in which external reality has been replaced by the protagonist's unconscious. His theater of the unconscious comprises fragmentary episodes involving fragmentary people, who appear briefly to proclaim the misery of their isolation, then disappear or are transformed suddenly, and often grotesquely, into other characters who are in search of themselves. Even such incomplete identity as they have is questionable, since their lives are not original but rather a recycled version of materials from history and culture. The pamphlet narrator, for example, finds himself a freak of evolution, having overdeveloped his attractive powers of intellect in order to compete with more virile men for the female of the species. He is all head and no body, a fragment of a person. Janey Davenport's scrap of identity is derived from the debris of her culture. Her thoughts, as she stands before the window of her room in Paris, reveal her as a synthetic version of romance magazines. Her fall to her death in the street below is a bathetic undercutting of her notion of love, and it is deflated further by the fact that she is then run over by a car. These characters sense that they do not exist, are merely actors performing on an empty stage; and their doubts of their existence are focused dramatically in the final scene in which Balso attempts to affirm his identity through a sexual act. The futility of this act strips him of his last illusion of uniqueness and importance, exposing him as the dupe of biological forces which do not recognize his claim to personal identity.

West's fiction is, as Auden points out, "absolutely self-centered," but this self-centeredness is complicated by the fact that his characters suffer from a radical lack of identity. They do not have meaningful external existences, nor do their inner lives lend themselves to a rewarding scrutiny, as in the case of the characters of Henry James. No authentic external or internal framework exists by which West's characters can find a sense of self-integration or wholeness, and they are, therefore, all trapped within themselves, or rather within their nonselves. Life is reduced to inhumanness, collisions of characters who cannot love, and who commit physical or psychic violence upon others in retaliation for the violence done to them. The sense of alienation in *Miss Lonelyhearts* consists of pure fear, terror, and helplessness, rendered partly in comic terms. The novel has a specific setting, New York City at the beginning of the thirties, but as a social community, the city hardly exists. West's characters have all been dehumanized, are locked into their anomic anxieties that are like violent states of stress. Those who write letters to Miss Lonelyhearts protest not only their misfortunes but also the misery of their fragmentation. This crisis is true particularly of Miss Lonelyhearts and Shrike, who feel the threat to their sense of existence most acutely, and enact quasi-religious roles, as Christ and Antichrist—obsessional delusions by which they are enabled, barely, to cope with the irrational nature of the world.

In one of the great moments of the novel, Mary Shrike is stripped naked by Miss Lonelyhearts before her apartment door, while she mutters incoherently that her father was a painter who misused her mother, and that her mother died of cancer of the breast, fragments of a past that she uses to shield herself from the emptiness of her own existence. More even than in *Balso Snell*, sexuality is the focus of the absurdity in *Miss Lonelyhearts*. Fay and Pete Doyle are a study in contrasts. She is absolutely vacant in her sexual assertion, and he is absolutely vacant in his sexual failure. Their relationship is one of misshapen individuals who meet under conditions of radical violence.

A Cool Million is an anatomy of dehumanization, but it is West's least successful novel partly because its political theme is a distraction, is not at all at the center of the interests that made West write fiction. These interests come out much more fully in *The Day of the Locust*, where sexuality is a focal concern. The novel once again reveals West's use of distortion and grotesquerie, but it is notable most of all for its sense of people who are destitute of real existence. Faye Greener is another of West's "inhuman" characters, and has been associated with a sexuality that incites incoherent outbursts of violence in the men who circle about her. Homer Simpson is incoherent to begin with; his progress through the work is a movement from a counterfeit existence in Wayneville, Iowa, where he is submissive and gropingly gentle, to his final giving way to sexual violence that is an expression of his repressed hatred of himself and others. His murder of Adore is, ironically, what he finds in place of the identity toward which he had groped. The other characters are like Homer in that they, too, cannot be redeemed into any meaningful existence.

Critics have often pointed out that West's heroes belong to a picaresque tradition, inasmuch as they are searchers in novels that develop episodically. Each novel has the form of a quest, but the quest leads to failure and frustration, since there is no objective reality on which West's characters can build. Outward reality has been "deconstructed" and shown to be absurd. Strangely, for a writer as nihilistic as West, an almost religious element enters into the works. His characters struggle toward some absolute truth, like Kafka's, only to be confronted by the horror of emptiness in their Godless worlds. The comedy of apocalypse is appropriate for West, since he writes of final things, and is appalled by mundanity and limitation.

Although West seems to disavow his Jewishness, he is in some respects closer to a Jewish tradition, particularly in his comic, quasi-religious seeking, than his writing might at first suggest. The *schlemiel*, the frequent butt of Jewish humor, provides the archetype for West's heroes, despite their putative Anglo-Saxon names. The comedy of the *schlemiel*, as Ruth R. Wisse notes in her study of the archetype,[2] is "existential." He is not merely a bumbling figure whose misfortunes come about by accident. His misfortune is his character, which compels him to suffer in a world that is as radically imperfect as he is. A victim, his fear is transformed into farce. He must laugh, or the reader must laugh at him, to keep from tears. Fear is the dominant emotion of West's humor, a fear so great that it escalates, finally, toward apocalyptic laughter.

No one has yet attempted an adequate comparison between the humor of West and his brother-in-law S. J. Perelman, who began their careers at the same time. The writing of both has been compared to cubist painting, and to surrealism, although it is not surrealist in any exact sense. Both are farceurs whose humor makes sudden, startling transitions from the elevated to the bathetic; and there is an element of violence in their work (in Perelman, in his assaultive, incongruous wordplay). Perelman's comic persona is that of a vain, mean-spirited man who is essentially weak, and is exposed in his vulnerability so that he, like West, is a victim. But one other feature they share is that they have conspicuously distanced themselves from their Jewish backgrounds. Known to all his friends as "Sid," Perelman in print employed the double initials "S. J.," in the tradition of the English man of letters. His style is consciously cultured (almost scholarly in its awareness of literature and love of arcane word usage) and cosmopolitan—the furthest remove from the image of that time of the urban Jew.

But if West and Perelman tended to cloak their Jewish themes and sensibilities in a partial accommodation to the expected standards of their time, Henry Roth did not. Roth, of course, was not a humorist, and there are, in fact, few writers who possess so little humor as he. But Roth can be compared to West as an American Jewish writer of the same period who was in some ways related to West in sensibility, and who expressed that sensibility in very specific Jewish terms. His novel *Call It Sleep* (1935) is set on New York's Lower East Side, where Jewish immigrants struggle for survival and with considerable anguish attempt to assimilate themselves into their new American life. A major influence on *Call It Sleep* is Joyce, particularly in *Ulysses*, which has the form of a journey into the inner life. In Roth's case, this journey is cast in the form of the nightmarishly overwrought imagination of a small Jewish boy in the city. The novel is realistic in many ways, yet its landscape is that of a dream. Fear and self-laceration are its most conspicuous features, a protracted torment of suffering that is never lightened by the slightest trace of humor. As with West's male characters, the paralysis of fear suffered by the boy is related to sexual anxiety, and his panic can neither be assuaged nor escaped. At the end his hysteria culminates in a long, intense, and poetic fantasia of apocalypse. Roth's apocalypse, it ought to be noted, is ultimately ambiguous. It is not clear, exactly, what it means. It is religious in intensity, yet no God is implied to exist in the world Roth has imagined with a pronounced naturalistic and Freudian emphasis.

In his essay "The Breakthrough: The American Jewish Novelist and the Fictional Image of the Jew,"[3] Leslie Fiedler has remarked that "Jewish American fiction in the 'thirties, whether specifically 'proletarian' or not, is characterized by [a] frantic religiosity without God, [a] sense of the holiness of violence." Roth's apocalyptic ending exemplifies this tendency toward a religious texture of emotion in a Godless world, but West's anguished questers also seem relevant. Noting a "flight from Jewish self-consciousness" in West's work,

Fiedler asks "in what sense is West a Jew at all?"; and he concludes that West's Jewishness is revealed in his quasi-religious seeking, and in his emphasis upon violence as a protest of lacerated innocence and of the incapacity of the sheltered Jewish boy to accommodate himself to the brutality of the world:

[West] is racked, that is to say, by guilt in the face of violence, shocked and tormented every day in a world where violence is daily. In *Miss Lonelyhearts*, he creates a kind of portrait of himself as one [who is] all nerves and no skin, the fool of pity whom the quite ordinary horrors of ordinary life lacerates to the point of madness. . . . [he] is the inventor for America of a peculiarly modern kind of book whose claims to credence are perfectly ambiguous. One does not know whether he is being presented with the outlines of a nightmare endowed with a sense of reality or the picture of a reality become indistinguishable from nightmare. For the record, it must be said that the exploiters of such ambiguity are typically Jews: Kafka for the continent, West for us.[4]

West's remarkable influence on later writers has often been noted, but the subject has as yet still not been fully explored. Marcus Smith, in his unpublished doctoral dissertation, "The Art and Influence of Nathanael West,"[5] discusses West's relation to Saul Bellow, Vance Bourjaily, Ralph Ellison, John Hawkes, Joseph Heller, Norman Mailer, Bernard Malamud, Flannery O'Connor, J. D. Salinger, and Bernard Wolfe; but even this account is incomplete. It does not note, for example, West's anticipation of, if not actual influence upon, the Theater of the Absurd. West's nonevolving characters, who must suffer mutely in their "absurd" circumstances, have a distinct affinity with the characters in Beckett's plays, who cannot evolve to the point of self-recognition or to a mastery of themselves or the world. West's characters are seekers of truth and understanding, but because the world, in its darkly enigmatic nature, is infinitely more powerful than they are, their search has the effect of reducing them to clown figures. West's vaudeville of inhumanness has, in this respect, very strong affinities with Beckett's tragi-comedies. In *Waiting for Godot*, the protagonists are tramps, homeless and placeless men who search for but cannot find identity or a sense of wholeness in their lives. Just as Miss Lonelyhearts, in his quest for transcendence, becomes the butt of many deflating comic incidents, Beckett's Vladimir and Estragon become the butts of crudely deflating physical humor. And just as Miss Lonelyhearts attempts to communicate with the other characters unsuccessfully, only to be driven further inward upon himself, so Beckett's protagonists talk at cross-purposes and are locked increasingly into their own isolation. In both cases, one finds a kind of echo chamber of mockery at the expense of those who seek the pure, the good, and the true. The sense of personal isolation is profound in West's novels, as it is again in Beckett's stark existential comedies; and this impression is deepened by the stylization of the characters as actors in an absurdist drama.[6]

Miss Lonelyhearts, to use him as an example again, so overacts his life that he is reduced to a set of theatrical gestures rather than becoming humanly related to those around him. Shrike, Shrike's wife, Pete Doyle, and Betty all play parts rather than participate in life with a sense of coherent relationship to one another. The same is true of West's other novels. Shagpole Whipple and Lemuel Pitkin in *A Cool Million* are not merely two-dimensional, since the stylized parts they play, at either end of the spectrum, as victimizer and victim, make them less than human. The characters in *The Day of the Locust*—Harry Greener and Faye, Abe Kusich and Homer—are "theatrical" conceptions. They are so intensely focused, so dramatized in the fixity of their limited natures, so much without relation to one another, that they can never come to larger consciousness and must always fail to establish contact. The characters in Beckett's plays, as well as those of Ionesco and Genet, give a similar sense of such enclosure within synthetic identities that they are less fully dimensional people than "performers" on an irrational stage.

The special quality of the laughter in West's novels can be noticed again in the work of Beckett, where one laughs with a wince, with the recognition that the comedy is at one's own expense, and involves final things, the unreasonable nature of existence itself. In Beckett's novel *Watt*, one of the characters tells the protagonist that there are three kinds of laughs:

. . . the bitter, the hollow and the mirthless . . . the bitter laugh laughs at that which is not good, it is the ethical laugh. The hollow laugh laughs at that which is not true, it is the intellectual laugh. Not good! Not true! Well well. But the mirthless laugh is the dianoetic laugh, down the snout—Haw!—so. It is the laugh of laughs, the *risus purus*, the laugh laughing at the laugh, the beholding, the saluting of the highest joke, in a word the laugh that laughs—silence please—at that which is unhappy.[7]

The comedy of West and Beckett has unhappiness inevitably as its subject—not merely that of particular individuals but of the larger unhappiness involved in the nature of the human condition itself.

More often noted is West's affiliation with the "grotesque" school of American fiction that emerged in the 1940s and 1950s. Together with other writers, including Sherwood Anderson and Faulkner, West provides a context for the grotesque conceptions of Carson McCullers. McCullers's brilliant first novel *The Heart Is a Lonely Hunter* (1940), published the year of West's death, portrays a world in which there is no communication between people, and in which representative characters are mutes. Her emphasis in the novel upon oddity and deformity is associated with sexual estrangement in *Reflections in a Golden Eye* (1941), which also employs a very strong homosexual theme, as does her story "The Ballad of the Sad Cafe" (1951), in which a central figure is a homosexual dwarf, a kind of extension of West's hunchback and dwarf misfits.

In the case of the grotesque fiction of Flannery O'Connor, one can speak of direct influence. In his introduction to *Everything That Rises Must Converge*, Robert Fitzgerald recalls that the only novels O'Connor urged on him during her stay in his Connecticut home were *Miss Lonelyhearts* and *As I Lay Dying*; and he adds that "it is pretty clear from her work that they were close to her heart as a writer."[8] In the 1960s, Stanley Edgar Hyman drew a parallel between the situations of West and O'Connor as writers, each having a "multiple alienation" from the dominant assumptions of their cultures: "he was an outsider as a Jew, and doubly an outsider as a Jew alienated from other Jews; she was comparably an outsider as a woman, a Southerner, and a Roman Catholic in the South." Hyman goes on to speak of West's effect on O'Connor's early fiction, particularly her first novel *Wise Blood* (1952). "The writer who most influenced her, at least in the first books," he remarks,

is Nathanael West. *Wise Blood* is clearly modelled on *Miss Lonelyhearts* . . . and contains many specific reminiscences of it. Hazel Motes has a nose "like a shrike's bill"; after he goes to bed with Leora Watts, Hazel feels "like something washed ashore on her"; Sabbath Lily's correspondence with a newspaper advice-columnist is purest West; and all the rocks in *Wise Blood* recall the rock Miss Lonelyhearts first contains in his gut and then becomes the rock on which the new Peter will found the new church.[9]

In his book *Nightmares and Visions—Flannery O'Connor*

and the Catholic Grotesque, Gilbert H. Muller agrees
with Hyman that West's is the most pervasive influence
on *Wise Blood*, adding: "Resemblances between the two
books [actually] exceed those enumerated by Hyman.
Four of the fourteen chapters in *Wise Blood* appeared as
short stories between 1948 and 1952, and in one of them,
'The Peeler,' Asa Hawkes is called Asa Shrike. Throughout the first half of Miss O'Connor's frequently
reworked novel this ostensibly blind fanatic is the main
adversary of Hazel Motes, just as Shrike is the scourge of
Miss Lonelyhearts. Moreover, the very fact that the
chapters in *Wise Blood* are self-contained episodes
suggests a basic structural similarity with West's book.
Both rely on the frame technique of the comic strip."[10]
Most strikingly of all, Miss Lonelyhearts and Hazel
Motes (men who have, by the way, the names of women)
develop Christ fixations, Miss Lonelyhearts delusively,
Motes reluctantly but in the end powerfully. Both novels
are concerned with grotesque characters, many of them
deformed, who exist in a tragicomic world of violence.

The relationship of West and O'Connor is complicated by the effect of both of them on John Hawkes. In
his article "Notes on the Wild Goose Chase,"[11] Hawkes
links West with O'Connor as writers who "created"
modern comedy through a humorous treatment of
extreme violence. "The true purpose of the novel,"
Hawkes remarks, "is to assume a significant shape and to
objectify the terrifying similarity between the unconscious desires of the solitary man and the disruptive needs
of the visible world," and he argues that West made this
objectification. "For Nathanael West," he writes, "love is
a quail's feather dragged to earth by a heart-shaped drop
of blood on its tip."

In an interview with John Graham,[12] Hawkes again
called attention to West and O'Connor as his literary
antecedents. "Nathanael West, I think," he told Graham,

"did make use of the sick joke, but I think he uses the sick joke always so that you feel behind it the innocence and purity, truth, strength and so on. This is at least implied . . . a larger desperate joke that is in, say, West's work. Nathanael West, Joseph Heller, Flannery O'Connor. All of these are, I think, comic writers dealing in extreme violence. If something is pathetically humorous or grotesquely humorous, it seems to pull us back into the realm, not of mere conventional values but of lasting values."

Hawkes's lengthiest discussion of West and O'Connor appears in his essay "Flannery O'Connor's Devil,"[13] in which he acknowledges that he was introduced to the fiction of Flannery O'Connor at the same time that he discovered the novels of Nathanael West:

At that time [in the early 1950s] the sudden confluence of West and Flannery O'Connor to me suggest twin guffawing peals of thunder . . . above a dead landscape quite ready for a new humor, new vision, new and more meaningful comic treatments of violence. . . . West is the one writer who, along with Flannery O'Connor, deserves singular attention as a rare American satirist. I would propose that West and Flannery O'Connor are very nearly alone today in their pure creation of "aesthetic authority," and would also propose, of course, that they are very nearly alone in their employment of the devil's voice as vehicle for their satire or for what we may call their true (or accurate) vision of our godless actuality. Their visions are different. And yet, as we might expect, these two comic writers are unique in sharing a kind of inverted attraction for the reality of our absurd condition.

Hawkes's three pieces provide a remarkable instance of a modern writer's definition of himself and his work through two earlier writers of related sensibility. What Hawkes notes about West and O'Connor invariably reflects his own aesthetic allegiances and approach to irrational comedy–particularly his notion of aesthetic autonomy, which dispenses with the usual conventions of realistic fiction to create a "pure" fiction of final things that becomes a way of understanding reality.[14]

Another later American writer indebted to West is Edward Lewis Wallant, who died in his mid-thirties in 1962, leaving behind four short novels. Both West and Wallant were deeply read in Dostoyevsky, and in their fiction are concerned with a Dostoyevskian inner crisis. Their heroes reach out for some form of transcendence in their self-enclosure and misery, and are surrounded by odd, unhappy, sometimes deformed characters who mirror their own condition. A striking difference between the heroes of West and Wallant is that Wallant's do finally achieve a breakthrough into human commitment. Sol Nazerman, in *The Pawnbroker* (1961), is a good example. A Polish Jew who has survived the horrors of a Nazi concentration camp, he lives a self-enclosed, "counterfeit" existence as a pawnbroker in Harlem. He cannot commit himself to others, until at the end, with the death of his assistant, a black who is significantly named Jesus, he is "born again" into life, achieves a redemption into human brotherhood.

Wallant's *The Tenants of Moonbloom* (1963) is less laden with symbolism than *The Pawnbroker*, but it tells a similar story. Norman Moonbloom, as a rental agent and building superintendent in New York for his more successful brother Irving, has reached a point of despair. He is oppressed by the meaninglessness of life rather like Miss Lonelyhearts. Miss Lonelyhearts receives letters entreating advice from the miserable and hopeless, and Norman Moonbloom is surrounded by such people in his daily rounds through the tenements he manages. These characters include a hunchback; an old Russian Jew who lives in indescribable filth; a "gnome" named Louie who lives in cramped quarters under the roof of his building;

and a candy-butcher named Sugarman who survives only
by his incessant clowning. They are versions of Dostoyevsky's wretched ones—and West's. And like West's
Miss Lonelyhearts, Norman Moonbloom, in his isolation, becomes a Christ figure. He experiences an illness
near Christmas time and emerges from it with a sense of
messianic mission. Miss Lonelyhearts's messianic mission begins in delusion and ends in death, but Norman
Moonbloom is permitted a happier fate. He breaks
through finally into life.

In his study of Wallant, David Galloway frequently
notes the similarity between West's fiction and Wallant's,
and in a closing passage remarks:

> Throughout this study, parallels have been suggested be-
> tween the writings of Edward Lewis Wallant and Nathanael
> West. Fate suggests yet more: both were Jews, each published
> four novels, both died as they seemed to be reaching the peak of
> their creative energies—West at thirty-seven and Wallant at
> thirty-six. They were intrigued by the nightmare of contempo-
> rary experience, and by the cripples and eccentrics who fight for
> existence in this ever-thinning air, armored with flimsy dis-
> guises and weaponed only with their brittle dreams. The two
> were also quintessentially comic writers, though West's laugh-
> ter was brittle and apocalyptic, while Wallant's was increasingly
> a versatile instrument of joy. The ambiguous confrontations of
> good and evil, the inevitability of suffering, the role of dreams
> and the concept of the "sick soul" were concerns they shared,
> and ones strongly reinforced, philosophically refined, by their
> readings of Dostoevsky.[15]

In other works West can be made out as a background
presence. Evelyn Waugh's *The Loved One* (1948), for
example, is reminiscent of *The Day of the Locust* in its
evocation of the empty horrors of Hollywood. Waugh's
English writers who come to make their livelihoods in
Hollywood share a sense of lost identity with the novel's

other characters. Juanita del Pablo, employed at one of
the studios, is being turned into an "Irish" actress, an
identity that is about as authentic as Homer Simpson's
cottage. Waugh's theme of failed identity, furthermore, is
linked with death, as in West. *The Loved One* moves from
the Hollywood studios, which represent a form of death,
to scenes of embalmment at a Los Angeles mortuary,
where the hero is greeted by a young woman with the
words "Mortuary Hostess" on her smock. Indeed, Whispering Glades Memorial Park is a Hollywood version of
death, cosmetically "beautified" and made unreal. Canned
music is piped through loudspeakers hidden in the shrub-
bery of the grounds, one section of which contains a plot
for writers that is a grotesque imitation of British literary
shrines. Mr. Joyboy, senior mortician at Whispering
Glades, has an embarrassingly obvious mother complex
and can express "love" only by the happy expressions he
gives to the faces of corpses whom he prepares for the
grave or the crematorium. The jest of *The Loved One*,
like that of *The Day of the Locust*, is that Hollywood is a
kind of living death.

   The Day of the Locust also seems influential on Robert
Stone's prize-winning first novel *A Hall of Mirrors* (1967).
Set in New Orleans, *A Hall of Mirrors* concerns a set of
maimed and displaced individuals who are drawn into a
world of nightmare. Events impel them toward a climactic "Patriotic Revival," where anarchy erupts. The scene,
in its wildness and incoherence, is reminiscent of the conclusion of *The Day of the Locust*, protracted in length and
reimagined in terms of the counterculture's clash with the
right-wing establishment of the 1960s. In an interview,
Stone acknowledged that in his adolescence West had
been a favorite author, and his influence was quickly
noted by a number of reviewers. Fred Rotondaro, for
example, remarked: "the nightmare quality of the work,
the confusion of values, and specifically the riot which

ends the novel, remind me of Nathanael West's *The Day of the Locust*. And just as with Tod Hackett in *Locust*, Rheinhardt goes mad at the end of his tale, screaming out at that which violates his humanity."[16]

More importantly, West is one of the recognized progenitors of the "black humor" writers of the 1960s. Bruce Jay Friedman, Terry Southern, and Jules Feiffer have all been cited as heirs of West in this humor of the irrational. Kurt Vonnegut's *Slaughterhouse-Five* (1969), with its inhuman violence and mad comedy, and Joseph Heller's *Catch-22* (1961), in which violence and irrationality are projected with the blackest satire against a World War II setting, may be placed in a line of descent from West's work. Walker Percy's *The Moviegoer* (1961), with its existential sense of American life as media illusion, has affinities with West; and such other writers as James Purdy, Thomas Berger, Donald Barthelme, John Barth, and Ralph Ellison have a contextual relationship to him. In particular, West's special relationship to Thomas Pynchon, a major sixties satirist, has been frequently noted.

Although Pynchon works on a vastly larger scale than West, his reduction of external reality (including history) to absurdity renders the individual as powerless and helpless as West's protagonists. In *V.* (1963), Pynchon's narrative consists of episodes from history since 1899, which are played off against episodes in the lives of contemporary American characters whom Pynchon calls the Whole Sick Crew. In this counterpointed narrative, historical episodes focus upon events of chaos and violence that lead up to or are involved in two world wars, while the contemporary scenes focus upon wild parties leading to violence and exhaustion. In either case, as Tony Tanner notes in *A City of Words*, there is a "tendency for people to regard or use other people as objects, and, perhaps even more worryingly, for people to regard themselves as objects. . . . The general falling away from the human whch is underway is underlined by the transformation in the lady V. In her appearances she becomes gradually less human and more composed of dead matter. When she is finally dismantled, it is suggested that she was found to be composed of entirely artificial objects."[17] This conception is similar to West's notion of "entropy" in *Miss Lonelyhearts*, man's losing battle with inertia and deadness; and it is worth noting that Pynchon's parodies of previous writers who have treated the inertia theme include West himself. But West is brought to mind most strongly in the passages in *V.* that are devoted to Benny Profane, who roams the fringes of the Whole Sick Crew, and can find nothing to give his life a sense of reality. The peculiar combination of gloominess of subject matter with geniality of satire is also reminiscent of West in Pynchon's more concise *The Crying of Lot 49* (1965), which deals with the disappearance of the American Dream; with the "cheated" ones who seek, often in paranoid fashion, to understand the cause of their meaningless lives.

West also played a seminal role in the development of American Jewish fiction after World War II. Edward Lewis Wallant, a latter-day interpreter of West, has been mentioned, but many other Jewish writers have a relation of one kind or another to him. Saul Bellow suggests West at times in his protagonists who are *schlemiels*, or suffering martyrs. From *The Victim* (1947) to *Herzog* (1964), Bellow's heroes are always at the verge of becoming Lemuel Pitkins, yet manage to hold on to their humanity. Augie March himself is constantly threatened with martyrdom or with an extinction of his identity, yet in the face of the most overwhelming odds drives through toward affirmation.

The problem of identity also enters into the work of another Jewish writer with whom West has been compared, J. D. Salinger. Salinger's Glass family has a privatist "religious" orientation, irregularly related to Zen, that is ultimately unclassifiable and stands outside of received Christian or Judaic orthodoxy, giving them a Westian unrelatedness. His characters in *The Catcher in the Rye* (1951) are particularly perplexing, since they have been drawn not as Jews but as WASPs who live comfortably on New York's East Side. Despite his putative gentile credentials, Holden Caulfield doesn't "fit in," and it is as if, all along, he has been playing a false role, which leads to his breakdown of identity. This breakdown makes him perceive the world around him, in almost paranoid fashion, in terms of an all-pervasive falsity. There is no love in it, and there is no communication between people that can withstand the stress of reality. In the end, like West's heroes, Holden becomes an outsider who has no system of belief to cling to, and can only suffer passively like Christ, or be driven to the edge of insanity.

In Philip Roth, uncertainty of identity results in endless variations of comic suffering that in one form or another is related to his characters' Jewish backgrounds. In *Goodbye, Columbus* (1959), Roth writes as a parodist of the newly-monied Jewish family, and examines the estrangement of a young hero who would marry into it. His earliest gift, like West's, is for satire and parody–a parody that has to do specifically with the unstable nature of his characters' sense of themselves. In *The Great American Novel* (1973), Roth parodies the "great American novel," the American Dream, baseball, and other icons of American mythology, as West had once parodied American ideals of community and oneness in *A Cool Million*. But principally Roth is related to West in his grotesque parodies of sexuality and the fulfillment it is supposed to offer. More specifically, Roth is concerned, even to the point of obsession, with male sexual fear. West's initial conception of *The Day of the Locust*, as has been mentioned, was to have included both a seven-foot lesbian and a male dwarf. The conception was later modified, but it is revealing that the sexes as represented in this notion should be a giantess and a tiny man. Comically, but frighteningly at times, too, Roth pits his vulnerable Jewish males against threatening women.

Roth's *Portnoy's Complaint* (1969) is a comically self-lacerating portrait of a young Jewish man who is dominated even in adulthood, kept small and childlike, and made neurotic, by his mother. His stunting and willful commitment to inner suffering give him strong affinities with West's protagonists, and reveal a similar kind of humor. Like West's, Roth's range has been somewhat limited, since his novels tend to be variations of a few themes. *My Life as a Man* (1974), for example, reveals another protagonist threatened by castration, not by his mother, but by his wife (who is, in a way, a version of the mother). In *The Breast* (1972), a Kafkaesque tale of metamorphosis, Roth's hero becomes transformed into a huge breast, losing the last vestige of his masculinity as he is swallowed up by femininity in a comedy of sexual ambivalence. In later novels, like *The Professor of Desire* (1977), Roth's protagonists continue to be reminiscent of West's stunted characters who cannot resolve their inner conflicts. Of the modern American Jewish novelists, Roth most closely resembles West in his role of satirist of the man who is immobilized by his sexuality and his perplexing relationship to the world without. What is merely implied in West, however, is examined by Roth as a very explicitly Jewish "problem."

The relevance of West to modern American humor extends even to nightclub and film comics, particularly two Jewish ones, Lenny Bruce and Woody Allen. Lenny Bruce's "black humor" makes one think of West in the sadism of his assault on the audience's nerves, his stripping away of appearances to reveal the loneliness and

ugliness of existence. The other half of West's
sadomasochism can be observed in the films of Woody
Allen, whose film persona is that of the Jewish male who
is anxiously uncertain of himself and is constantly
humiliated, either in fact or in his inner fears. Allen's
is the comedy of self-laceration. Even his intelligence,
his "culture," cannot help him; instead it adds to the
number of ways he can torture himself with his mis-
givings—including, certainly, a fear of sexual inadequacy.
He becomes another comic victim who, like West's
protagonists, is essentially passive and committed to
suffering.

An analogy might be drawn between the careers of West
and John O'Hara, both of whom were preoccupied by
isolation and estrangement when they began as novelists
in the early part of the 1930s. Both were attracted to satire
and irony, were influenced by F. Scott Fitzgerald, and
came to have a special relationship to him. And both published their most notable novels, *Appointment in Samarra*
and *Miss Lonelyhearts*, at an early stage of their careers.
O'Hara became the supreme short story writer of his
time, and attracted a vast following. He proved to be
enormously prolific, and although his later novels were of
uneven quality, they sold in the millions of copies and
made him known to the whole reading public of his time.
West's career was almost the reverse of O'Hara's. He
produced, in all, only four short novels, earned very little
from them, and by the time of his early death was known
only to a limited number of readers. By the 1960s, however, West came to enjoy a posthumous fame and exerted
an extraordinary influence on a new generation of American writers, while O'Hara's reputation among critics
declined sharply. O'Hara was considered by American
tastemakers to be out of touch with the sixties, his dense
social realism and centrist allegiances an anomaly in a time

preoccupied by more radical envisionings of the universe. West, by contrast, became the thirties innovator who was perceived as a forerunner of almost everything. Their days of favor were reversed.

West's world was never large; like the brevity of his books, his short sentences and scanty paragraphs, it was pinched and reduced in scale. He was a miniaturist whose special subject was miniaturity in life, the failure of his characters to evolve or to attain coherent identity. In college, West drew grotesque doodles and cartoons, and later as a novelist he became a cartoonist of loneliness and anguished isolation. The distinctive quality of his fictional cartooning was its savagery. In his pages American life was reduced to a maze of mirrors reflecting illusion, and offering no basis for positive belief. He absorbed the pessimism and skepticism of the European modernists, and extended a twenties alienation into the Depression period. Marxist novelists and critics of the thirties always felt uncomfortable with West, despite his support for leftist causes, since his fiction, in all of its implications, was inimical to their commitment to social reconstruction. But he did manage to portray the Depression, on his own terms, with great fidelity. The absolute collapse of values, the sense of a deep and enormous betrayal of the individual, left maimed and incoherent, all record the shock of that experience, and could even be termed a form of protest.

West's mockery was directed especially at sexuality, which in his fiction was pictured as a form of violence. To West's perception, the life of the nation consisted of nothing *but* violence, and as a corollary sexuality and violence became indistinguishable. At times, as in *A Cool Million*, he weakened his case against sexuality as an extension of national violence by forcing his theme. But at his best, he was a detached and compelling witness of sexual horror. In *Miss Lonelyhearts* and much of *The Day*

of the Locust, he created a poetry of cruelty, allied to sexual drives, that is informed by a disturbing sense of "evil."
West wrote against the grain of American optimism, the
malignant sexuality he recorded cutting away at the dark
underside of the nation's fantasy life. Mass dreaming and
the fantasy life of the country as it twists into torment
were his special subjects, as much as sexuality itself.

West was equipped with a generous amount of
neurosis, and as a novelist he was limited in many ways,
as Auden has noted. He had only one theme, the loss of
identity, and he did not envision it with many variations.
But in *Miss Lonelyhearts* he produced one of the enduring
fictional masterpieces of modern times. He was an outsider with a special gift for imagining cripples, grotesques
who became his Everyman figures; and they were
imagined by him so luminously that he taught others a
new way in which to see themselves. His subject was
dark, and even gross, but he infused it with the charm of
his humor. Few writers have ever written of horror with
such gaiety.

Notes

1. NATHANAEL WEST: THE SHAPE OF THE LIFE

1. Details of West's career have been drawn from James F. Light's *Nathanael West: An Inerpretative Study* (Evanston, Illinois: Northwestern University Press, 1961), a pioneering critical biography, and Jay Martin's *Nathanael West: The Art of His Life* (New York: Farrar, Straus & Giroux, 1970), a more modern and detailed treatment. Martin's biography can be faulted in some respects, particularly in its lack of focus and sharpness, but in the fullness of its background detail it is indispensable for anyone concerned with West's career. It is the major background source for this study.

2. S. J. Perelman was elected editor of the campus humor magazine, *The Brown Jug*, in 1924, and after graduating the following year was a regular contributor and cartoonist for *Judge* magazine in New York City from 1925 to 1929. He was cartoonist and writer for *College Humor* magazine during 1929–1930, and from 1931 onward was a frequent contributor to *The New Yorker*. His pieces for *The New Yorker* provided the material for the nearly forty books that he published during his lifetime. Perelman married West's sister Laura in the summer of 1929, and the Perelmans preceded West to Hollywood, where, at the beginning of the thirties, Perelman wrote the films *Monkey Business* (1931) and *Horse Feathers* (1932) for the Marx Brothers.

West was not the only writing member of the Weinstein family, since Laura, in collaboration with her husband, wrote for the stage and for films, and was at one time on the executive board of the Screenwriters Guild. With Perelman, she wrote the stage comedies *All Good Americans* (1933) and *The Night Before Christmas* (1941), which had brief runs in New York; and she collaborated with him on the screenplays *Florida Special* (1936), *Ambush* (1939), *Boy Trouble* (1939), and *The Golden Fleecing* (1940). Laura died at the ninety-one acre farm at Erwinna, Pennsylvania, in 1970, and Perelman died in 1979. For a concise account of Perelman's career, see Douglas Fowler, *S. J. Perelman* (Boston: Twayne, 1983), particularly chapter four, "Perelman and the Tradition," pp. 84–108, a discussion of Perelman's writing in relation to Jewish humor.

3. James F. Light, *Nathanael West*, p. 33.

4. West's pessimism has also been noted by those who knew him in Hollywood. Budd Schulberg asked a woman who had worked in Stanley Rose's bookstore as a young girl, and is now a well-known literary agent in Hollywood, for her impressions of West, and she replied: "Sad. Everything about him was sad. And melancholy. Strange. Remote. Detached. . . . At the same time . . . he was terribly warm and friendly, but in a strange, detached way. Oh, and gentle. I remember him as terribly gentle." Budd Schulberg, *Writers in America: The Four Seasons of Success* (New York: Stein & Day, 1972; revised 1983), p. 167.

5. A fictional treatment of West's life and career, written after his death, appears in Herbst's "Hunter of Doves," *Botteghe Oscure*, XIII (1954), 310–44. Herbst's Jamesian nouvelle deals with the deceased Westian author Noel Bartram whose real name had been Alec Barber, and who in the 1930s had written three short novels that were "the sum of his art." A Mrs. Heath, his friend and confidante, is approached by a young man from Boston, who is interested in writing a biography of him. In the course of the story, Bartram's associations are brought out–his sister Nora, a "softer shadow of his own nature," and her husband Joel Baker, his friend in college and always after "his inseparable friend." The young biographer queries Mrs. Heath about Bartram's life as manager of a small hotel, and his years in Hollywood, but at the end Mrs. Heath is unable to supply him

with the answers about Bartram that he seeks. She tells him of Bartram's social presence ("his shyness, alertness, and gift of seeing"), and of his created world, having "the nightmarish quality of an intense dream," but cannot locate the link between the two. Who and what, she asks, "had ruled Bartram's dream world?" The young biographer is confronted by a Bartram who is beyond explanation, and leaves Mrs. Heath with a sense of frustration. Herbst wrote reminiscently of West again in her reverential essay "Nathanael West," *Kenyon Review*, XXVIII (Autumn 1961), 611–30. For further information about Herbst's friendship with West, see Elinor Langer's recent biography *Josephine Herbst* (Boston: Atlantic/Little, Brown, 1984).

6. Moss and Kamin also suggested that William Carlos Williams revive the magazine *Contact*, which he had edited with Robert McAlmon in 1920–21. In 1931 the magazine was reissued, with Williams as editor and West as associate editor, and with an editorial policy that emphasized a native American tradition rather than the more remote one of Pound and Eliot. They particularly encouraged the local, colloquial, and brutal—what West called "American superrealism." Their first issues were represented by Williams, West, Perelman, Cummings, James T. Farrell, John Herrmann, and Yvor Winters; but because they were unable to pay contributors, or to attract the writers they most wanted, the magazine's life ended with the third issue. Williams continued to be a special admirer of West's work, and after West's death, when *The Day of the Locust* was reprinted in 1950, wrote: "Had he gone on there would have unfolded, I think, the finest prose talent of our age."

7. When Lillian Hellman and Dashiell Hammett stayed as West's guests at the Sutton Hotel in the autumn of 1932, they were at the turning points of their respective careers. It was at the Sutton that Hellman began her first play, *The Children's Hour*, the idea for which had been suggested to her by Hammett. *The Children's Hour* was produced on Broadway in 1934, and immediately made Hellman famous. Hammett at this time was at work on *The Thin Man* (1934), the most commercially successful of his detective novels but a falling off in quality from

his earlier books. Thereafter, although making large amounts of money in Hollywood, Hammett was never again able to write another major work. By the late forties, both Hellman and Hammett were in trouble with congressional committees investigating "subversives" in Hollywood. Hellman was blacklisted in the film industry for many years, and Hammett served a penitentiary sentence as an "uncooperative witness." See Hellman, *An Unfinished Woman* (Boston: Little, Brown, 1969); *Pentimento: A Book of Portraits* (Boston: Little, Brown, 1973); and *Scoundrel Time* (Boston: Little, Brown, 1976). For biographies of Hammett, see Richard Layman, *Shadow Man: The Life of Dashiell Hammett* (New York: Harcourt Brace Jovanovich, 1981); William Nolan, *Dashiell Hammett: A Life at the Edge* (New York: Congdon & Weed, 1983); and Diane Johnson, *Dashiell Hammett: A Life* (New York: Random House, 1983).

8. Published at Chapel Hill, North Carolina, *Contempo* had a notable list of contributors that include Kay Boyle, Ezra Pound, Sherwood Anderson, Hart Crane, John Dos Passos, Theodore Dreiser, William Faulkner, Wallace Stevens, and William Carlos Williams. West met its editor, M. K. Abernathy, at Moss and Kamin's bookstore in New York, and thereafter corresponded with him. "Miss Lonelyhearts in the Dismal Swamp," a first draft of chapter 8 of *Miss Lonelyhearts*, was published in *Contempo*'s July 5, 1932, issue. The symposium on *Miss Lonelyhearts* appeared in its May 15, 1933, issue, with commentary on West by Angel Flores, S. J. Perelman, Josephine Herbst, Bob Brown, and William Carlos Williams, accompanied by West's own piece "Some Notes on Miss L."

9. The 1933 film version of *Miss Lonelyhearts*, retitled *Advice to the Lovelorn*, starring Lee Tracy, bore almost no relation to West's novel. The protagonist is a tough, fast-talking reporter in the Ben Hecht style who is assigned as punishment to the "sob-sister" desk, where he uncovers the murder mystery with which the film is actually concerned.
Miss Lonelyhearts was adapted for the Broadway stage in 1957 by Howard Teichman—a production that was directed by Alan

Schneider, and that starred Fritz Weaver as "Miss L," and Pat O'Brien as Shrike. It received generally unfavorable notices. Henry Popkin, who reviewed it for *Commonweal* (October 25, 1957) under the title "The Taming of Nathanael West," found it a travesty of West's book. "It comes alive rather fitfully," Popkin commented, "when we hear violent, stinging, often blasphemous lines written by West; but even their force is lost because they are mostly in the mouth of Miss Lonelyhearts' hard-boiled editor, whose diabolism is mitigated by a late conversion and by the genial Irish humor that Pat O'Brien imparts to the role. The cynicism is hollow, the anguish is unfelt, and the play is aimless. . . . What West's savage, violent, grotesque book required was a savage, violent, grotesque adaptation and production."

West's novel was adapted for the screen a second time, in 1959, as *Miss Lonelyhearts*. Produced by Dore Schary as a quality film, it starred Montgomery Clift as Miss Lonelyhearts, Dolores Hart as his girl friend Betty, Maureen Stapleton as Fay Doyle, Robert Ryan as editor Shrike, and Myrna Loy as Mrs. Shrike. The film was reviewed by Dwight Macdonald (*Encounter*, XIII, July 1959, 51–55), who wrote: "I greatly admire West's novel, which seems to me a miraculously pure expression of our special American sort of agony, the horror of aloneness, and of our kind of corruption, that of mass culture. [But] this new production of *Miss Lonelyhearts*, for all its 'seriousness,' is just another soap opera. . . . Doyle does turn up at the newspaper office to shoot Miss Lonelyhearts, but he is so overcome by Our Hero's sincerity and compassion that he cannot pull the trigger and staggers out, a sadder and wiser man. Even the cynical Shrike, who up to this point has been handing out a poor man's equivalent of the novelistic Shrike's destructive rhetoric, suddenly has a change of heart and begs Our Hero to stay on the paper. When O. H., though 'deeply moved,' insists on leaving (*with* his girl, of course, whom he is about to marry, of course, and who, of course, happily explains as she exits, 'I believe in him'), Shrike gazes at O. H. will ill-concealed affection. . . . All the film has in common with the book is the name of its characters."

10. Quoted in James F. Light, *Nathanael West*, p. 103.

11. Alexander King, the well-known book illustrator (and later humorist) founded *Americana* magazine in 1932 as a broadside attack on American civilization and its "miasmic stench." Contributors to the first issue included George Grosz, Jose Clemente Orozco, John Sloan, E. E. Cummings, Gilbert Seldes, William Steig, and James Thurber. West's brief association with George Grosz, the savagely satiric German artist who had recently come from depression-ridden Germany, is of interest, since Grosz's origins, like West's, were in dada and surrealism. His best work, done in the Weimar period, has no parallel, in the ferocious nature of its satire, in the US. His drawings are comic yet deeply horrifying, and evoke men as mindless robots, creatures of lust, greed, and depraved appetites. "After It Was Over They Played Cards" (1917) shows men playing cards after they have dismembered a female victim; and "The Little Murderer" (1918) portrays a drunken man attacking a nude woman with a knife. A number of his drawings depict street scenes that include gaunt, leprous-looking prostitutes, and stout men with lumpy genitals that wrinkle their clothes. In "Pandemonium" (1914), a scene of riot takes place in which a horrible looking man leeringly fondles a nude woman, and is similar in some ways to West's crowd scene in *The Day of the Locust*. For a concise account of Grosz's career, see John I. H. Baur, *George Grosz* (New York: Macmillan, 1954); for a detailed account of his major period, see Beth Irwin Lewis, *George Grosz: Art and Politics in the Weimar Republic* (Madison, Wisconsin: University of Wisconsin Press, 1971).

12. James F. Light, *Nathanael West*, p. 108.

13. Ibid.

14. Although purchased by Columbia Pictures in 1934, *A Cool Million* was never produced as a film. In 1937, with Samuel Ornitz, West incorporated elements of *A Cool Million* into his screenplay *It Could Happen to You*, about the rise of fascism in America. Although produced and released, the film did very

poorly at the box office. Again, in late 1939, with Boris Ingster, West wrote an "adaptation" of *A Cool Million*, related hardly at all to the novel, which was sold to Columbia Pictures. But it, too, was unproduced. Terry Southern, who co-wrote the film *Doctor Strangelove*, is said to be preparing a screen adaptation of *A Cool Million* at the present time.

15. West's work as a screenwriter in Hollywood has been detailed in Tom Dardis, *Some Time in the Sun* (New York: Scribner, 1976), pp. 151–82, and, more fully, in Martin's *Nathanael West*, which includes an annotated appendix, "Nathanael West's Film Writing," pp. 401–6. The films on which West worked principally are: *Beauty Parlor*, Columbia Studios, 1933, unproduced; *Return to the Soil*, Columbia Studios, 1933, unproduced; *Ticket to Paradise* (with Jack Wattleford), Republic Productions, 1936; *Follow Your Heart* (with Lester Cole and Samuel Ornitz), Republic Productions, 1936; *The President's Mystery* (with Lester Cole), Republic Productions, 1936; *Gangs of New York*, Republic Productions, 1936–37; *Jim Hanvey–Detective*, Republic Productions, 1936; *Rhythm in the Clouds*, Republic Productions, 1937; *Ladies in Distress*, Republic Productions, unproduced; *It Could Happen to You* (with Sanuel Ornitz), Republic Productions, 1937; *Orphans of the Street*, Republic Productions, 1937–38; *Stormy Weather*, Republic Productions, 1937–38, unproduced; *Osceola*, an unassigned "original" treatment, 1935, unproduced; *Broadway Bible*, an unassigned "original" treatment for a musical screenplay, 1938, unproduced; *The Squealor*, Columbia Studios, 1938, unproduced; *Five Came Back* (with Jerry Cady and Dalton Trumbo), RKO Pictures, 1938, released 1939; *Flight South*, retitled *Heritage of the Wind* (with Gordon Kahn and Wells Root), MGM, 1938, unproduced; *The Spirit of Culver* (with Whitney Bolton), Universal, 1939; *I Stole a Million*, 1939; *The Victoria Docks at Eight*, Universal, 1939, unproduced; *Before the Fact* (with Boris Ingster), RKO Pictures, 1939; *Men Against the Sky*, RKO Pictures, 1940; *Let's Make Music*, RKO Pictures, 1940; *Stranger on the Third Floor*, RKO Pictures, 1940; *A Cool Million* (with Boris Ingster), Columbia Studios, unproduced; *Bird in Hand* (with Boris Ingster),

RKO Pictures, 1940, unproduced; *Amateur Angel* (with Boris Ingster), Columbia Pictures, 1940, unproduced.

16. Quoted in Jay Martin, *Nathanael West*, p. 306.

17. *Good Hunting* was West's single produced stage play. He conceived the idea for the play in 1937, after reading a book on the outmoded methods of warfare of English military strategists, and soon interested Joseph Schrank in collaborating with him. The play, written chiefly by West, was accepted for presentation by the producer Jerome Mayer in 1938. It opened in November of that year, with Mayer himself directing, at the Hudson Theatre in New York. The play was a dark comedy about the professional class of British military officers who are out of touch with reality. Their complacent assumptions of "good taste" and old-school methods lead to a series of grotesque debacles and horrible defeats. The failure of West's antiwar play was blamed partly on the shift in public opinion in the US, as the country moved from an isolationist to a more internationalist stance; but Mayer's direction was also considered a liability. Primary responsibility for the failure of the play, however, rests with West's script, which the audience failed to find amusing. The sound of a single man laughing in the otherwise total stillness of the theater suggests the perplexed reaction of those who went to see it. The text of *Good Hunting* has never been published.

18. By 1940 West was planning to take an extended leave from Hollywood to work on a new novel, the plot of which was just forming in his mind. It would involve a reporter who writes a regular column on the "absurdity of the actual." At one point, he notices an advertisement soliciting members for the Golden Friendship Club, which was to have provided the novel's plot. The "friendship club" refers to an organization which, for a fee, puts lonely people in touch with each other, its ads in large newspapers and magazines sandwiched in between "panaceas for acne endorsements and for miracle-working electric belts." "All over the country," West wrote in his notes, "thousands of helpless and depressed souls in dingy bedrooms and faraway

farms, read these ads and dream [of overcoming their unhappi-
ness]. . . . It is on these tragic creatures that friendship clubs
prey." See Martin, pp. 394–96.

19. Quoted in Jay Martin, *Nathanael West*, p. 11.

20. S. J. Perelman, "Nathanael West: A Portrait," *Contempo*, 3
(July 25, 1933), 1–4; reprinted in Jay Martin, *Nathanael West:
A Collection of Critical Essays* (Englewood Cliffs, New Jersey:
Prentice-Hall, 1971), pp. 11–12.

2. *The Dream Life of Balso Snell:*
WEST'S THEATER OF THE UNCONSCIOUS

1. Breton's "humour noire" is the reverse of the genial, having
the irrational, cruel, mocking quality of surrealism. For Breton's discussion of "humour noire," see his *Anthologie de
l'humour noire* (1940). Eugene Ionesco later used the term to
describe his own kind of theatrical "comedy" in *La démystifica-
tion par l'humour noire* (1959). "Humor makes us conscious,
with a free lucidity," he remarked, "of the tragic or desultory
condition of man. . . . Humor is the only possibility we possess
of detaching ourselves–yet only after we have surmounted,
assimilated, taken cognizance of it–from . . . the malaise of
being. To become conscious of what is horrifying and to laugh
at it is to become master of that which is horrifying. . . . We
have become aware. . . . The true nature of things, truth itself,
can be revealed to us only by fantasy, which is more realistic
than all the realisms." Quoted in Martin Esslin, *The Theatre of
the Absurd* (Garden City, New York: Doubleday, rev. ed.,
1969), p. 158.

2. Randall Reid, *The Fiction of Nathanael West: No Redeemer,
No Promised Land* (Chicago: University of Chicago Press,
1969), pp. 15–16.

3. The earliest fragment of *Finnegans Wake* (1939) to be published in periodical form appeared in the April 1924 issue of the
transatlantic review. Chapter 5 of the "Work in Progress"
appeared in *Criterion* in July 1925, and five fragments of the

work were published serially in September 1926. Eugene Jolas published sections of the novel in *transition* on a regular basis from April through November 1927, after which publication became more sporadic. West and his friends held lengthy discussions of Joyce and *transition* in the late 1920s; and in 1931 West attended group discussions of literature and the arts at the apartment of George Brounoff, where regular sessions were devoted to the analysis of *Finnegans Wake*.

4. Quoted in James F. Light, *Nathanael West*, p. 41.

5. West's attraction to vaudeville began early in life, and was a lasting interest. As a youth, he attended performances at vaudeville and burlesque houses on 125th Street in Harlem. By the twenties, according to Martin, "he had a wide acquaintance with the conventions of burlesque comedy," and was "an accomplished aficionado of the standard routines." In the early thirties, he went to Harlem nightclubs with Robert Coates, who shared his interest in vaudeville, and at this time West frequently spoke of burlesque comedy as classical in form. He talked to Martin Levy in a "scholarly and accurate way" of the connection between burlesque and Greek comedy, knew the "standard routines and traced them to *The Birds* and other plays." In Los Angeles, West knew a number of performers in the Follies Burlesque, and sometimes took Levy backstage to meet them.

6. The Trojan horse, whose interior might suggest a womb, has been interpreted as a maternal symbol by James F. Light, who refers the reader to chapter 2, "The Battle of Deliverance from the Mother," in Jung's *Psychology of the Unconscious* (1916). He notes that "much might be done with Jung's discussion of the horse, especially the Trojan Horse, as a maternal symbol: into it man enters out of a wish to be reborn; from it he emerges not as a child but as a man." He feels that the "maternal" horse implies "not only West's rejection of Judaism, but also his rejection of the mother." Light, *Nathanael West*, p. 53.

7. Randall Reid, *The Fiction of Nathanael West*, p. 39.

8. Kingsley Widner, *Nathanael West* (Boston: Twayne, 1982), p. 22.

3. *Miss Lonelyhearts:*
THE ABSURD CENTER OF THE DEAD WORLD

1. The "Susan Chester" letters, kept by West and later made available to Martin, are discussed in *Nathanael West: The Art of His Life*, pp. 110, 187. Curiously, certain details in the letters to Miss Lonelyhearts that give the impression of having been invented by West have some basis in the letters themselves. One woman wrote that she was "stooping to put the broom under the bed to get the lint and dust . . . lo-behold I saw a face which resembled the mask of a devil—only the whites of his eyes and hands clenched ready to choke anyone." The woman signed herself "Broad Shoulders," adding, "Susan, don't think I am broad shouldered. But that is just the way I feel about life and me." Her name, "Broad Shoulders," and the incident of the man under the bed, were incorporated by West into the longest and most disturbing letter Miss Lonelyhearts receives. West's method, generally, was to make the letters more illiterate, increasing the effect of the writers' helplessness, and to make their contents more unsettling. A sixteen-year-old girl, for example, had written to "Susan Chester" of her weak knee that made her walk with a slight limp; but in the letter in the novel, the girl, more disturbingly, has no nose.

2. The chapters are: "Miss Lonelyhearts and the Lamb," *Contact*, 1 (February 1932): 80–85; "Miss Lonelyhearts and the Dean Pan," *Contact*, 1 (May 1932): 13–21; "Miss Lonelyhearts and the Clean Old Man," *Contact*, 1 (May 1932): 22–27; "Miss Lonelyhearts in the Dismal Swamp," *Contempo*, 2 (July 5, 1932): 1–2; "Miss Lonelyhearts on a Field Trip," *Contact*, 1 (October 1932): 50–57. The serial chapters are reprinted in William White, *Nathanael West: A Comprehensive Bibliography* (Kent, Ohio: Kent State University Press, 1975), pp. 132–62. Critical articles on West's revisions are: Carter A. Daniel, "West's Revision of *Miss Lonelyhearts*," *Studies in Bibliography*, 16 (1963): 232–43; reprinted in Jay Martin, ed., *Nathanael West: A Collection of Critical Essays* (Englewood Cliffs, New Jersey: Prentice-Hall, 1971), pp. 52–65; and

Robert I. Edenbaum, "To Kill God and Build a Church: Nathanael West's *Miss Lonelyhearts*," *CEA Critic*, 29 (June 1967), 5–7, 11; reprinted in Thomas H. Jackson, ed., *Twentieth Century Interpretations of Miss Lonelyhearts: A Collection of Critical Essays* (Englewood Cliffs, New Jersey: Prentice-Hall, 1971), pp. 61–66.

3. Nathanael West, "Some Notes on Miss L.," *Contempo*, 3 (May 15, 1933): 1–2; reprinted in William White, *Nathanael West: A Comprehensive Bibliography*, pp. 165–66; and in Jay Martin, ed., *Nathanael West: A Collection of Critical Essays*, pp. 66–67.

4. Nathanael West, "Some Notes on Miss L.," in Martin, ed., *Nathanael West: A Collection of Critical Essays*, p. 66.

5. John O'Hara's *Appointment in Samarra* (1934) was published only a year after *Miss Lonelyhearts*, and it, too, belongs distinctively to the American Depression period. Different as they are, the novels have certain features in common, since they are tautly written, brilliantly controlled anatomies of particular American locales of the early thirties. Each is concerned with misery, loneliness, and the loss of identity in a society in which meaning can no longer be located, and where all things end in a trauma of sexuality. *Appointment in Samarra* takes place during the three days of the Christmas holiday, and an absent Christ broods over its scene of violence and despair; and in *Miss Lonelyhearts*, Christ is called upon and petitioned, but only a sordid confusion is revealed. Death is a common theme, and both heroes become increasingly disoriented in the course of the works, losing their lives at the end. Both novels are symptomatic of what Josephine Herbst called "a Great Distress."

6. In the early 1930s, West met frequently with a group of young Jewish intellectuals to discuss music, literature, and politics at the apartment of George Brounoff on Central Park West. According to Martin, Dostoyevsky "inevitably provided the major ideals for the group. They read all his works in translation and were especially influenced by *The Brothers Karamazov*, but

also by *A Raw Youth, The Idiot, The Possessed,* and *Crime and Punishment.* . . . The kind of Christ figure or secular saint which they found in Prince Myshkin appealed strongly to them as the highest development, along certain lines, of their own ideals." (Martin, p. 114). West, however, mocked the sentimental idealism of the group before his Village friends, and insisted that people were victims, who used ideal figures such as Christ to conceal their condition from themselves. Dostoyevsky, nevertheless, remained one of West's major literary interests, and he read his novels over and over during the course of his life. The dramatic and strongly scenic construction of Dostoyevsky's novels, and his preoccupation with intense inner states of conflict, influenced West significantly.

7. Randall Reid, in *The Fiction of Nathanael West*, pp. 50–52, has compared Miss Lonelyhearts to Raskolnikov in some detail. He comments: "Both Raskolnikov and Miss Lonelyhearts are, when we meet them, already launched on an obsessive idea whose genesis is only hinted at. In both, the obsession ambiguously reflects a personal illness and a real external problem–it is simultaneously true that Miss Lonelyhearts is driven by 'hysteria' and that he is driven by a clear perception of the misery of others. In both cases, the external problem is the fact of apparently hopeless suffering. And in both cases, the resulting obsession focuses on the necessity of an heroic action–Raskolnikov imitates Napoleon; Miss Lonelyhearts imitates Christ. The heroic action raises a series of questions: Is the action desirable? Is the hero capable of it? Are his apparent motives real? Raskolnikov and Miss Lonelyhearts alternately doubt the action itself and their own worthiness to attempt it. . . . Both are . . . poised between mocking antagonists and loving but incomprehending girls."

8. West's incorporation of *The Waste Land* into *Miss Lonelyhearts* has been noted in the past by Edmond L. Volpe, "The Waste Land of Nathanael West," *Renascence*, 13 (1961), 69–77, 112; reprinted in Thomas H. Jackson, ed., *Twentieth Century Interpretations of Miss Lonelyhearts*, pp. 81–92; and by Victor Comerchero, *Nathanael West: The Ironic Prophet*

(Syracuse, New York: Syracuse University Press, 1964), 86–88.
Volpe regards *Miss Lonelyhearts* as a more negative version of
The Waste Land, since at the end of his poem Eliot offers qualified hope, while West denies that any is possible. Comerchero
focuses upon the Grail quest theme, viewing Miss Lonelyhearts
as a searcher who hopes to renew the blighted land.

9. The only critic in the past to have commented on *The Great
Gatsby* and *Miss Lonelyhearts* is Randall Reid, pp. 98–99. Reid
remarks: "The triad of Doyle, Mrs. Doyle, and Miss
Lonelyhearts recalls the similar grouping of Wilson, Myrtle
Wilson, and Gatsby in *The Great Gatsby*. In both novels, a
crippled or devitalized cuckold is married to a vulgar but vital
woman, and in both novels the cuckold mistakenly kills the
'spiritual' hero in revenge for his wife's betrayal. . . . Even the
styles of Fitzgerald and West are related. Both write with an
acute ear for vulgar speech, with an instinct for poetry and comedy. I think West learned from Fitzgerald, and I think the
grotesque fate of Miss Lonelyhearts was a conscious echo of
Gatsby's grotesque end."

10. There are even very specific moments in *Miss Lonelyhearts*
that are reminiscent of Fitzgerald's novel. Pete Doyle's physical
gestures are not synchronized with his speech, and his features
do not compose to form any coherent whole, so that his face is
"like one of those composite photographs used by screen
magazines in guessing contests." His facial incoherence is similar
to that of Myrtle Wilson's sister Catherine in *The Great Gatsby*,
since her face, too, has a blurred and incoherent quality. The
descriptions occur at the beginning of scenes of radical confusion and squalor. In another passage, Miss Lonelyhearts "was
conscious of two rhythms that were slowly becoming one.
When they became one, his identification with God was complete." The lines recall the passage in *The Great Gatsby* in which
Gatsby confuses Daisy with God, and at their lips' touch "the
incarnation was complete."

11. Pound's translation of Li Po's "Lament of the Frontier
Guard" is a "wasteland" poem that focuses upon desolation and

a sorrow from which there is no escape. The "gracious spring" of the poem has turned into an autumn of suffering and isolation, making it apt in connection with the little park, where Miss Lonelyhearts meditates in the spring that cannot arrive, and where his burden cannot be lightened.

12. R. W. B. Lewis, *Trials of the Word: Essays in American Literature and the Humanistic Tradition* (New Haven: Yale University Press, 1965), pp. 213–14.

13. Stanley Edgar Hyman, *Nathanael West* (Minneapolis: University of Minnesota Press, 1965), p. 23.

14. Nathanael West, "Miss Lonelyhearts and the Lamb," *Contact*, February 1932; reprinted in William White, *Nathanael West: A Comprehensive Bibliography*, p. 133.

15. V. S. Pritchett, *The Living Novel & Later Appreciations* (New York: Random House, 1964), p. 279.

4. *A Cool Million:* THE VAUDEVILLE OF APOCALYPSE

1. The manuscripts of West's unfinished stories were made available to Martin, and quotations from the stories come from his biography. West's unfinished stories are: "The Adventurer" (Martin, pp. 35–37, 166–68); "The Fake," later entitled "L'Affair Beano," and finally "The Impostor" (Martin, pp. 88–90); "Mr. Potts of Pottstown" (Martin, pp. 168–70); "The Sun, the Lady, and the Gas Station" (Martin, pp. 171–72); "Three Eskimos" (Martin, p. 213); "Tibetan Night" (Martin, pp. 170–72); "Western Union Boy" (Martin, pp. 41–42, 55, 268–69).

2. Long before *A Cool Million*, W. D. Howells had employed the theme of Lemuel Gulliver as traveler into the irrational in his novel *The Minister's Charge, or the Apprenticeship of Lemuel Barker* (1887). Howells's Lemuel is a poor country boy who journeys to Boston with the mistaken notion that he will find a stable social order and a place for himself within it. What he finds instead is a world in which the certainties of the past have been shaken and are disappearing, and in which the individual must

confront his own very "modern" isolation. West does not seem to have been conscious of Howells's novel in writing *A Cool Million*, but some parallels exist, especially the mythic quality of the young man's quest and the reversal of his expectations. Both Lemuel Barker and Lemuel Pitkin are fatherless New England boys from the country who come to the big city to seek their fortunes, like Alger's heroes; and it seems likely that Howells had Alger in mind, at least partly, in his satiric treatment of the country-boy myth.

3. *Candide*, a cruel satire of a naive youth's encounter with the world, has been influential on both English and American fiction. Robert M. Adams, in his 1966 introduction to the Norton edition of Voltaire's novel, has noted its effect on "all the Evelyn Waugh and Aldous Huxley heroes, as well as Augie March, Holden Caulfield, Huckleberry Finn and all his multitudinous descendants."

4. Douglas H. Shepard, "Nathanael West Rewrites Horatio Alger, Jr.," *Satire Newsletter*, 3 (Fall 1965), 13–28.

5. Gary Scharnhorst, "From Rags to Patches, or *A Cool Million* as Alter-Alger," *Ball State University Forum*, vol. 21, #4 (1980): 58–65. Scharnhorst has also discussed Alger and his parodists in *Horatio Alger, Jr.* (Boston: Twayne, 1980). The parallel passages in Alger and West cited by Scharnhorst in his articles are: *Andy Gordon*, chapter 6, *Cool Million*, chapter 1; *Tom Temple's Career*, chapters 8–9, *Cool Million*, chapter 3; *The Erie Train Boy*, chapters 1–2, *Cool Million*, chapters 5–6; *Joe's Luck*, chapter 5, *Cool Million*, chapter 10; *Ben Bruce*, chapter 12, *Cool Million*, chapter 12; *Andy Grant's Pluck*, chapter 17, *Cool Million*, chapter 16; *Joe's Luck*, chapters 25–27, *Cool Million*, chapters 24–25.

6. Jay Martin, *Nathanael West*, p. 238. "The literary analogue of this novel, Poe's 'The Man Who Was Used Up,' makes clear that *A Cool Million* follows in the tradition of grotesque comedy, from Poe and Melville through Kafka and Gogol, rather than in the traditions of social or political satire."

7. Robert I. Edenbaum, "A Surfeit of Shoddy: Nathanael West's *A Cool Million*," *Southern Humanities Review*, 2 (1968), 427–39.

8. R. W. B. Lewis, *Trials of the Word*, p. 214. Lewis goes on to call *A Cool Million* "far more penetrating . . . than the rather hastily contrived image [of political apocalypse] which appeared the following year in Sinclair Lewis's *It Can't Happen Here*." *It Can't Happen Here* (1935) was, in fact, written in only four months, partly to exploit interest in the forthcoming presidential election; and it cannot be taken seriously as literature. None of its characters has any depth or believability, least of all Berzelius ("Buzz") Windrip, who becomes president and then dictator. Interestingly, however, Lewis's novel has a number of features in common with *A Cool Million*. The hero of *It Can't Happen Here*, Doremus Jessup, is an elderly newspaper editor who, like Lemuel Pitkin, is from Vermont. And "Buzz" Windrip is a paternalistic demagogue who appeals to the "know-nothing" element of the country, particularly to the lower-middle class, and has a constituency that is also Whipple's. The Hearst papers are alluded to in both novels, and in Lewis's work they support Windrip's candidacy. Just as in *A Cool Million*, the demagogue figure harps on the theme of the sinister combination of Jewish bankers and Bolsheviks as the wreckers of the country's ideals. As Whipple has his "leather shirts," Windrip organizes his Minute Men, or Storm Troops. Windrip even has a "Buzz" song that is similar in type to the "Lemuel Pitkin Song" in *A Cool Million*.

9. The parallel between Abraham and Isaac and Whipple and Lem is discussed by T. R. Steiner in "West's Lemuel and the American Dream," in David Madden, ed., *Nathanael West: The Cheaters and the Cheated: A Collection of Critical Essays* (Deland, Florida: Everett/Edwards, 1973), pp. 150–70.

10. R. W. B. Lewis, *Trials of the Word*, p. 214.

    5. *The Day of the Locust:* ABSURDISM IN HOLLYWOOD

1. Nathanael West, "Bird and Bottle," *Pacific Weekly*, 5

(November 10, 1936), 329–31. Reprinted in Martin, ed., *Nathanael West: A Collection of Critical Essays*, pp. 132–37.

2. Robert M. Coates, letter to Cyril Schneider, June 6, 1952; quoted in James F. Light, *Nathanael West*, p. 155.

3. Information about the composition of *The Day of the Locust* is drawn chiefly from Martin, *Nathanael West*, pp. 258–66, 311–15.

4. For more detailed comment on the title of *The Day of the Locust* and Scripture, see Nathan A. Scott, Jr., *Nathanael West: A Critical Essay* (Grand Rapids, Michigan: William B. Eerdmans, 1971), p. 32.

5. It has also been suggested by Walter Wells that Mr. Kahn's "Pleasure Dome" is a parody of the grinning face of Ikey Cohn, symbol of New York's Rockaway Playland amusement park. Walter Wells, *Tycoons and Locusts: A Regional Look at Hollywood Fiction of the 1930s* (Carbondale: Southern Illinois University Press, 1973), p. 55.

6. The comic episodes in *Sanctuary* (1931) are played off against scenes of murder, rape, and lynching, but provide more than comic relief, since they often have an ironic function. The beer (rather than tea) party at Miss Reba's house of prostitution, for example, is a burlesque of a morally bankrupt genteel society; and the wake for the gangster Red has a similar implication. At the wake, Red's corpse tumbles out of its coffin, dislodging a wax plug in its forehead to reveal a bullet hole, and is a kind of stripping away of polite pretensions to expose the horror and vacancy lying beneath. Everyone who has read *Santuary* remembers the comic episode in which Virgil Snopes and Fonzo Winbush, from Jefferson, Mississippi, arrive in Memphis and mistake Miss Reba's brothel for a boarding house. But there is a more muted humor in the fact that Temple Drake, the daughter of a judge and a pillar of society, should find her real vocation in the brothel–so much so that she scandalizes Miss Reba herself. If *Sanctuary* can be compared with West's work, it would be in

its dark, cartoonlike humor of emptiness. In Faulkner's novel, as in *The Day of the Locust*, the author's embitterment is related to women, who have an inhuman emptiness, and in whom the absurdity of the culture is reflected. Richard Chase has remarked that "Faulkner's novel offers . . . passages of humor that give it a place among the modern novels of grotesque comedy as practiced in various ways by Conrad, Kafka, Nathanael West, and others who have brought to the older comic tradition of Dickens and Dostoevski a modern or 'existential' tone." Richard Chase, *The American Novel and its Tradition* (New York: Doubleday–Anchor, 1957), p. 206.

7. A highly visual or cinematic novel, *The Day of the Locust* was adapted for the screen in 1975. The film was directed by John Schlesinger, with Waldo Salt as screenwriter, and starred Donald Sutherland as Homer, William Atherton as Tod, Burgess Meredith as Harry Greener, and Karen Black as Faye. The film received mixed reviews. Vincent Canby, in the *New York Times* (May 8, 1975), called it "a huge and in many ways remarkable film," but referred to the "almost lunatic scale on which Mr. Schlesinger has filmed its key sequences." Jay Cocks, in *Time* (May 12, 1975), remarked: "Schlesinger and Screenwriter Waldo Salt collaborated previously on *Midnight Cowboy*, and *The Day of the Locust* has much the same mood of sentimental surrealism. Both films treat rather bizarre subjects in a comfortably slick fashion, so that nothing becomes very real or threatening. . . . *The Day of the Locust* looks puffy and overdrawn. . . . [The riot] is skillfully and elaborately staged, but wildly overwrought. The announcer at the premiere is made up to look like Hitler, and his excitement drives the crowd to greater excesses of violence. It moves like a marauding army. Not only are people trampled and windows broken, but fires start, telephone poles fall, and Hollywood Boulevard seems to shake."

8. The Flemish painter James Ensor (1860–1949), who began his career shortly before 1880, was one of the major pioneers of modern art–an influence on the German expressionists of the 1920s as well as on the American Abstract Expressionists of the

1950s. His preoccupation with death and the grotesque sometimes took the form of carnival scenes haunted by skulls and by
individuals who wear horrible masks. Christ is a recurring
figure in Ensor's work, and in some of his paintings is shown
being tortured by demons. Josephine Herbst compared West's
novels to the paintings of Ensor, and Martin has elaborated
further on the analogy in *Nathanael West*, p. 316.

9. Nathanael West, "Burn the Cities" (1933), first published in
Martin, pp. 329–31.

10. The influence of Sherwood Anderson on *The Day of the
Locust* has been proposed by a number of critics, including
Daniel Aaron and William Van O'Connor, but Reid's discussion is by far the most detailed. Randall Reid, *Nathanael West*,
pp. 139–45.

11. Robert Phillips has also compared Fitzgerald's *Tender Is the
Night* to *The Day of the Locust* in his note "Fitzgerald and *The
Day of the Locust*," *Fitzgerald Newsletter*, #15 (Fall 1961), 2–3.
Phillips does not claim influence, but he does note a number of
parallels, including a masquerade motif and the idea of the death
of culture in a world of brutality. The Riviera setting of *Tender
Is the Night* is depicted as the "stage" of a dying world, and
when Rosemary Hoyt visits the film studio, she notices the
"bizarre debris of some recent picture, a decayed street scene in
India, a great cardboard whale, a monstrous tree bearing cher-
ries large as basketballs." The scene, as Phillips points out,
anticipates West's use of the studio sets to evoke falsity and illusion in the culture at large.

12. A number of works of the early thirties that are set in Hollywood—such as Raoul Whitfield's *Death in a Bowl* (1933) and
Paul Cain's *Fast One* (1933)—are crime novels, and do not
attempt to bring the Hollywood movie industry into focus,
except as a metaphor for an "open city," where money may be
made quickly and values are negotiable. Liam O'Flaherty's
Hollywood Cemetery (1935) and Eric Knight's *You Play Black
and the Red Comes Up* (1938) are more directly concerned with

the film industry, and two of Horace McCoy's hard-boiled novels touch on it—*They Shoot Horses, Don't They?* (1935) and *I Should Have Stayed Home* (1938). Gloria Beatty, one of the principal characters in *They Shoot Horses, Don't They?*, is a movie extra, and many of the characters in *I Should Have Stayed Home* earn their marginal livings in the same way. All are disillusioned by Hollywood and some are destroyed. But Cain's novels are crudeness itself compared to the more intricate art of West. Two of the better novels about Hollywood appeared only a year before *The Day of the Locust*—John O'Hara's *Hope of Heaven* (1938) and John Dos Passos's *The Big Money* (1938), the final installment of his *U.S.A.* trilogy.

13. Aldous Huxley's *After Many a Summer Dies the Swan* (1939) was published in the same year as *The Day of the Locust*, while *The Last Tycoon* appeared in 1941, with Budd Schulberg's *What Makes Sammy Run?* Other novels with Hollywood settings published in the forties include Evelyn Waugh's ghoulishly humorous *The Loved One* (1948) and Raymond Chandler's mystery *The Big Sister* (1949). Hollywood novels of the fifties include Schulberg's *The Disenchanted* (1950), inspired by Fitzgerald's Hollywood experience, William Saroyan's *Rock Wagram* (1951), Dos Passos's *Most Likely to Succeed* (1954), Norman Mailer's existentially pretentious *The Deer Park* (1955), and Wright Morris's study of nihilistic escapism *Love Among the Cannibals* (1957). More recent novels are Alison Lurie's brilliantly satiric *The Nowhere City* (1965) and Joan Didion's highly styled study in wasteland angst *Play It As It Lays* (1970). But there have been a great many others. For studies in the Hollywood novel, see Kingsley Widmer, "The Hollywood Image," *Coastlines*, 5 (1961), 17–27, and "The Last Masquerade," in David Madden, ed., *Nathanael West*, pp. 179–93; Carolyn See, "The Hollywood Dream Cheat," in David Madden, ed., *Tough Guy Writers of the Thirties* (Carbondale: Southern Illinois University Press, 1968), pp. 199–217; and Jonas Spatz, *Hollywood in Fiction* (The Hague: Mouton, 1969). All of these, however, are sketchy and incomplete, and there has as yet been no definitive study.

6. Conclusion

1. W. H. Auden, "West's Disease," in *The Dyer's Hand and Other Essays* (New York: Random House, 1962), pp. 238–45; reprinted in Jay Martin, ed., *Nathanael West: A Collection of Critical Essays*, pp. 147–53.

2. Quoted in Douglas Fowler, *S. J. Perelman*, p. 104.

3. Leslie A. Fiedler, "The Breakthrough: The American Jewish Novelist and the Fictional Image of the Jew," *Mainstream*, 4, #1 (Winter 1958), 15–35.

4. Ibid., pp. 21–22.

5. Marcus Smith, "The Art and Influence of Nathanael West." Doctoral Dissertation, 1964. The University of Wisconsin (Madison). *DAI*, v. 25, pp. 4155–56.

6. See Frank Shelton, "Nathanael West and the Theatre of the Absurd," *Southern Humanities Review*, v. 10, pp. 225–34. Shelton notes that "all the characters in West's novels are 'actors, poseurs' as are the stage characters in Samuel Beckett, Eugene Ionesco, and Jean Genet," and argues that "a striking and not merely coincidental congruence of theme and technique" can be traced between West and the stage absurdists.

7. Quoted in Nathan A. Scott, Jr., *Nathanael West: A Critical Essay*, p. 17. In this passage, Scott comments on the similarity of the passage in Beckett with the one in *Balso Snell* in which the pamphlet narrator speaks of "mocking laughter at its source," that is, the irrationality of life from which "pure" laughter springs.

8. Robert Fitzgerald, Introduction, Flannery O'Connor, *Everything That Rises Must Converge* (New York: Farrar, Straus, and Giroux, 1956, paperback reprint, 1970), xv.

9. Stanley Edgar Hyman, *Flannery O'Connor* (Minneapolis: University of Minnesota Press, 1967), pp. 43, 46.

10. Gilbert H. Muller, *Nightmares and Visions–Flannery O'Connor and the Catholic Grotesque* (Athens, Georgia: University of Georgia Press, 1972), p. 20. Muller also remarks: "Among the major writers of the thirties, the grotesque was a seminal impulse in the fiction of Faulkner and Nathanael West; and it continues to pervade the best contemporary fiction– Vladimir Nabokov, John Barth, James Purdy, John Hawkes, and Thomas Pynchon."

11. John Hawkes, "Notes on the Wild Goose Chase," *Massachusetts Review*, 3 (Summer 1962), 784–88.

12. John Hawkes, "John Hawkes on His Novels" (an interview with John Graham), *Massachusetts Review*, 7 (Summer 1966), 449–61.

13. John Hawkes, "Flannery O'Connor's Devil," *Sewanee Review*, 70, #3 (Summer 1962), 395–407.

14. Hawkes's critics have all noted West's influence, but see particularly Patrick O'Donnell, *John Hawkes* (Boston: Twayne, 1982), and Robert I. Edenbaum, "John Hawkes: *The Lime Twig* and Other Tenuous Horrors," *Massachusetts Review*, 7 (Summer 1966), 462–75–both of whom draw comparisons between Hawkes's *The Lime Twig* and *The Day of the Locust* as fantasies with sexuality at their core.

15. David Galloway, *Edward Lewis Wallant* (Boston: Twayne, 1979), p. 151.

16. Fred Rotondaro, *Best Sellers*, 27 (September 1, 1967), 217. In another review, Ivan Gold remarked: "*A Hall of Mirrors* is, one could say, *The Day of the Locust*, as told to Malcolm Lowry and edited by Frantz Fanon." Ivan Gold, *New York Times*, September 24, 1967, p. 4.

17. Tony Tanner, "*V.* and V-2," in Edward Mendelson, ed., *Pynchon: A Collection of Critical Essays* (Englewood Cliffs, New Jersey: Prentice-Hall, 1978), p. 17. Reprinted from Part I,

"Caries and Cannibals," in Tanner's *City of Words: American Fiction, 1950–1970* (London: Jonathan Cape; New York: Harper & Row, 1971), pp. 153–88.

Bibliography

I. BOOKS BY NATHANAEL WEST

The Dream Life of Balso Snell. New York: Contact Editions, 1931.
Miss Lonelyhearts. New York: Liveright, 1933.
A Cool Million. New York: Covici-Friede, 1934.
The Day of the Locust. New York: Random House, 1939.
The Complete Works of Nathanael West. New York: Farrar, Straus and Cudahy, 1957.

II. BOOKS ON NATHANAEL WEST

Comerchero, Victor. *Nathanael West: The Ironic Prophet.* Syracuse, New York: Syracuse University Press, 1964.
Hyman, Stanley Edgar. *Nathanael West.* Minneapolis: University of Minnesota Press, 1962. (Pamphlet)
Jackson, Thomas H., ed. *Twentieth Century Interpretations of Miss Lonelyhearts.* Englewood Cliffs, New Jersey: Prentice-Hall, 1971.
Light, James F. *Nathanael West: An Interpretative Study.* Evanston, Illinois: Northwestern University Press, 1961.
Madden, David, ed. *Nathanael West: The Cheaters and the Cheated: A Collection of Critical Essays.* Deland, Florida: Everett/Edwards, 1973.
Malin, Irving. *Nathanael West's Novels.* Carbondale: Southern Illinois University Press, 1972.
Martin, Jay. *Nathanael West: The Art of His Life.* New York: Farrar, Straus & Giroux, 1970.
————, ed. *Nathanael West: A Collection of Critical Essays.* Englewood Cliffs, New Jersey: Prentice-Hall, 1971.

Perry, Robert M. *Nathanael West's Miss Lonelyhearts: Introduction and Commentary.* New York: Seabury Press, 1969. (Pamphlet)

Reid, Randall. *The Fiction of Nathanael West: No Redeemer, No Promised Land.* Chicago: University of Chicago Press, 1967.

Scott, Nathan A., Jr. *Nathanael West: A Critical Essay.* Grand Rapids, Michigan: William B. Eerdmans, 1971. (Pamphlet)

Vannatta, Dennis P. *Nathanael West: An Annotated Bibliography of the Scholarship and Works.* New York: Garland, 1976.

White, William. *Nathanael West: A Comprehensive Bibliography.* Kent, Ohio: Kent State University Press, 1975.

Widmer, Kingsley. *Nathanael West.* Boston: Twayne, 1982.

III. Other Criticism

Aaron, Daniel. "Late Thoughts on Nathanael West," *Massachusetts Review*, 6, #2 (Winter–Spring 1965), 307–17.

———. "The Truly Monstrous: A Note on Nathanael West," *Partisan Review*, 14, #1 (1947), 98–106.

Auden, W. H. "West's Disease." *The Dyer's Hand and Other Essays.* New York: Random House, 1962, pp. 238–45.

Coates, Robert M. Introduction. *Miss Lonelyhearts.* New York: New Directions, 1950, pp. lx–xiv.

Cowley, Malcolm. Introduction. *Miss Lonelyhearts.* New York: Avon, 1959, pp. ii–lv.

Dardis, Tom. *Some Time in the Sun.* New York: Scribner, 1976, pp. 151–82.

Fiedler, Leslie A. "The Breakthrough: The American Jewish Novelist and the Fictional Image of the Jew," *Mainstream*, 4 (Winter 1958): 15–35.

Fowler, Douglas. *S. J. Perelman.* Boston: Twayne, 1983.

Gehman, Richard B. Introduction. *The Day of the Locust.* New York: New Directions, 1950.

Hawkes, John. "John Hawkes on His Novels," *Massachusetts Review*, 7 (Summer 1966), 449–61.

———. "Flannery O'Connor's Devil," *Sewanee Review*, 70, #3 (Summer 1962), 395–407.

Herbst, Josephine. "Hunter of Doves," *Botteghe Oscure*, 13 (1954), 310–44.

Lewis, R. W. B. "Days of Wrath and Laughter." *Trials of the Word*. Yale University Press, 1965, pp. 184–236.

———. "Hart Crane and the Clown Tradition," *Massachusetts Review*, 4 (Summer 1963), 745–67.

Pritchett, V. S. *The Living Novel and Later Appreciations*. New York: Random House, 1964, pp. 276–82.

Schulberg, Budd. *Writers in America: Four Seasons of Success*. New York: Stein & Day, 1983, pp. 162–86.

Wells, Walter. *Tycoons and Locusts: A Regional Look at Hollywood Fiction of the 1930s*. Carbondale: Southern Illinois University Press, 1973, pp. 49–70.

Wilson, Edmund. "The Boys in the Back Room: Postscript." *A Literary Chronicle: 1920–1950*. New York: Doubleday, 1950, pp. 245–49.

Index